CONTENTS

DEDICATION

To
Loretta Trezzo Braren
& Ken Braren
for bringing my books to life.

FABRIC SCRAPS:
Every Crafter's Challenge

Perhaps it's my Yankee roots, or that love for fabric inherent in quilters. Whatever it is, I simply can't forsake anything but the smallest leftover bit of fabric to the trash can.

Come to find out, I'm not alone. Recently, I noticed a quilter had posted this message on a computer bulletin board: "My husband retrieves the most minuscule fabric remains from the floor and asks me, 'Honey, should I put this one in the scrap box?'" Frugality can go to the extreme for sure!

Of course, we all save our scraps assuming the day will come when we find the perfect project for them. That day has finally arrived. In **Scrap Crafts**, you'll find useful objects and decorative items to keep, or to give as gifts, all with full-size patterns and step-by-step instructions.

These special crafts will be a welcome opportunity for you to put those long-neglected and ever-growing boxes of scraps to good use. By sifting through those bits and pieces, you'll take a journey along a time line of past quilting and sewing projects. Perhaps you'll sew new items to match some of the crafts completed months, or even years ago.

The very idea of decorative scrap crafts reflects a folk art sensibility. Making use of what's "free" at hand, coupled with an uncomplicated design sense, follows this tradition.

To make sorting all of these accumulated scraps easier, I organize my scraps by color into separate cardboard storage boxes. If you have a smaller assortment of scraps, shoe boxes or empty laundry detergent boxes, covered with contact paper, fabric, or wallpaper scraps, might be a better option.

The craft projects in this book use large and small scraps. A large scrap may be defined as an odd-shaped, quarter-of-a-yard piece left over from a past Halloween costume. For small pieces, you'll need to decide realistically whether you will ever have a need for that two-inch, odd-shaped scrap before saving it. If it is a favorite fabric or from a memorable creation, then, of course, you'll find a place to give it new life.

Whether by making an adorable folk art wooly lamb or a versatile braided scrap wreath, you're sure to make a small dent in your scrap collection and satisfy your frugal side, too. And most importantly, you will have created something that is certain to give lasting pleasure.

♥

Jodie Davis

GETTING STARTED

This chapter provides the fundamentals for constructing the projects in this book. It describes basic sewing equipment and provides a quick review of sewing techniques. For additional sewing know-how, the sewing reference books listed in the bibliography at the end of the book are excellent sources. You will find these references in your local library or bookstore.

Before you begin your project, assemble all the necessary tools and materials; then, follow the instructions one step at a time.

GENERAL SUPPLIES

Essential

Bent-handle dressmaker's shears: Good, quality shears, 7" or 8" in length, are recommended for general sewing purposes. Reserve these shears for cutting fabric only, as paper will dull them quickly.

Scissors: Used for cutting paper, cardboard, and other materials, these inexpensive scissors will save your shears from a lot of wear and tear.

Dressmaker's tracing paper: Used for transferring markings from patterns to fabric.

Dressmaker's tracing wheel: A device used with the tracing paper.

Straight pins or paper weights: To hold paper pattern pieces in place as you cut the fabric out.

Hand-sewing needles: For general hand sewing. Choose a fine, size 10-8, sharp for lightweight fabrics such as calico, and a medium, size 8-6, sharp for heavier fabrics such as corduroy, flannel, and denim.

General purpose thread: The all-purpose size 50 will fill most of your general hand- and machine-sewing needs.

Glue: A general purpose white glue made for fabric, felt, wood, and paper is available at any dime, crafts, or fabric store under a variety of brand names.

Paper: For patterns.

Nice to Have

Seam ripper: A sharp, pointed tool used to tear out temporary basting stitches and seams. I list this as nonessential because you can substitute the thread clippers instead.

Pinking shears: These cut a ravel-resistant zigzag. They are used for finishing seams. A good choice is the 7¹/₂" size.

Thread clippers: A variation on a small pair of scissors, thread clippers are made by a number of companies and are handy for trimming threads at the sewing machine, for clipping into seam allowances, and for making buttonholes. If you do much sewing, I highly recommend having a pair on hand.

Thimble: This is listed as nonessential though many, including myself, will argue that this little piece of equipment is essential in guiding the needle and guarding against painful pinpricks.

STITCH DICTIONARY

Running Stitch

This stitch is similar to the basting stitch, though it is a shorter, even stitch, for fine, permanent seaming.

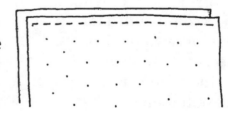

Basting Stitch

This long, ¹/₄" by hand or longest possible by machine, temporary stitch is used for marking and for stitching together two pieces of fabric to make sure they fit properly before the final stitching.

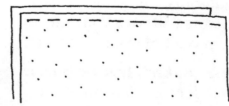

Topstitch

Longer than a regular sewing stitch, the topstitch is applied from the right side of the finished item. It is for decorative or functional purposes (to secure casings, zippers, facings).

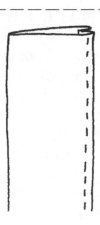

Ladder Stitch

Use this stitch to fasten two pieces of fabric invisibly, such as when closing openings after stuffing.

Whipstitch

This stitch is used to join two edges, such as the bottom edges of the teddy bears' ears.

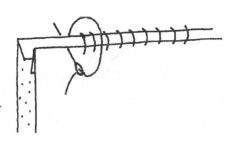

Satin Stitch

A closely spaced zigzag stitch, often used to cover the raw edges of appliques.

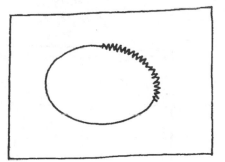

Gather Stitch

Long basting stitches used to gather fabric, often to match a larger piece of fabric to a shorter piece of fabric.

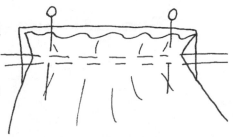

MAKING PATTERNS

With the exception of the "stained glass" pillows, all of the patterns in this book are shown in their actual size. Make the patterns out of scrap paper. Or, for a more durable pattern, use cereal boxes.

The easiest way to make the patterns is to duplicate them on a copy machine. Compare the copy to the original to be sure the copier has not distorted the image.

An even quicker method is to lay white paper over the pattern and trace.

How to Make Crazy Patchwork

Crazy patchwork is what scrap crafts are all about, and it's so easy to do!

INSTRUCTIONS

1. Lay the batting on top of the muslin.

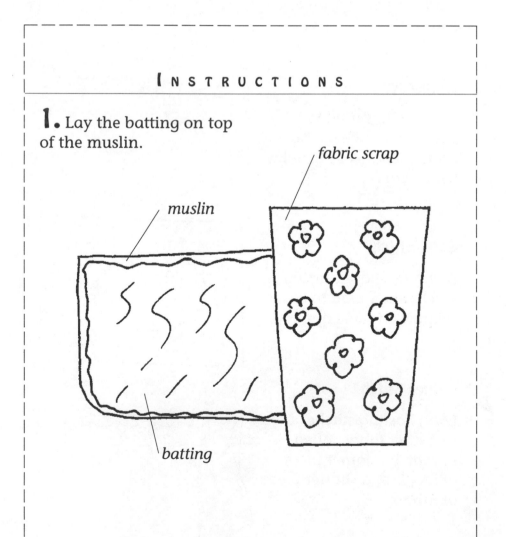

muslin

fabric scrap

batting

2. Piece the scraps over the batting/muslin as shown, stitching through all layers.

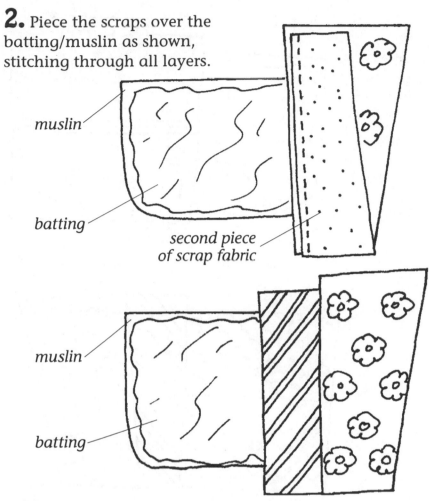

muslin

batting

second piece of scrap fabric

muslin

batting

3. To get perpendicular patches, piece two fabrics together first and then sew them over the batting/ muslin and pieced scrap pieces as shown.

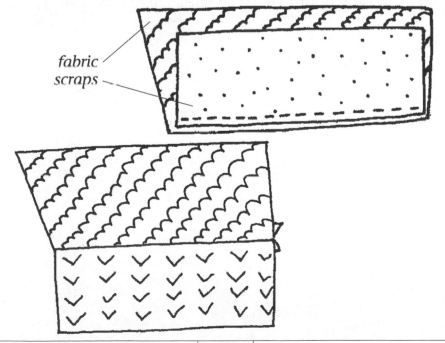

fabric scraps

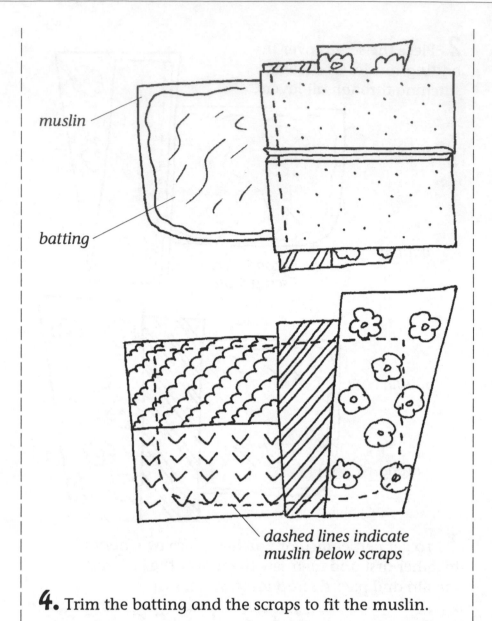

muslin

batting

dashed lines indicate
muslin below scraps

4. Trim the batting and the scraps to fit the muslin.

HOME DECORATION

BRAIDED WREATH

This colorful wreath is a snap to make and will add warmth to a baby's room or dress up any door in your home. It requires only three materials: a straw wreath base, some scrap fabric, and a few pleasurable hours!

MATERIALS

Fabric scraps in at least 20"-long pieces — the amount depends on the size of the wreath

Straw wreath

INSTRUCTIONS

1. Cut or tear the fabric into $\frac{1}{2}$"- to 1"-wide strips.

2. Temporarily fasten together (with a clothespin) the ends of three strips, two or three inches from the ends.

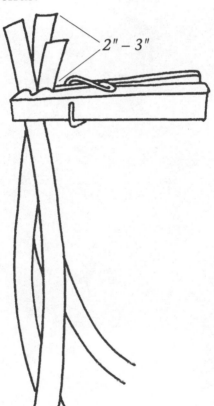

2" – 3"

Braid the three strips together. Remove the clothespin.

3. Holding one end of the braid in each hand, wrap it around the straw wreath so that the ends are along the outside edge of the wreath.

Tie the two ends of the braid together. Trim the ends to 2" to 3".

4. Repeat, adding braids all the way around the wreath until the straw wreath is filled with braids, as shown in the photograph.

HEART DESIGN QUILT

Finished size is 52" square.

A perfect beginner's project, this quilt is simply a grid of squares. The squares are sewn into strips, one for each vertical row of the quilt, and the strips are then sewn together to form the quilt top.

As a guideline for using scraps, or for your convenience if purchasing fabrics, yardages are given in the materials list. The fabric I chose for my border has a 6"-wide repeat. If your border fabric has a wider or narrower repeat, your quilt will be larger or smaller.

MATERIALS

2 yards fabric A

1 yard fabric B

¾ yard fabric C

⅝ yard fabric D

½ yard fabric E

½ yard fabric F

Scrap of fabric G

Scrap of fabric H

3½ yards backing fabric

Matching thread

2 yards border fabric

Approximately 60" square of batting

Quilting thread

INSTRUCTIONS

Note: All seam allowances are ¼" unless otherwise specified.

Prewash and iron your fabrics.

1. Cut the fabrics for the quilt top into 2½" squares according to the following chart. Stack them in piles and label them A,B,C, and so forth.

Fabric Key to Quilt Piecing Diagram

SYMBOL	FABRIC	NUMBER OF SQUARES
	A	244
	B	108
	C	82
	D	51
	E	38
	F	38
	G	3
	H	12

2. To form the quilt top, piece the squares into vertical strips and then stitch the strips together.

Referring to the Quilt Piecing Diagram on page 24 and the fabric key, start piecing your quilt top in the top left corner. Piece two background squares, row 1, column 1 and row 2, column 1 together. These are both Fabric A pieces.

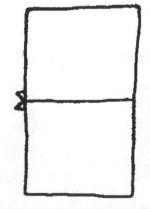

Add the third piece, row 3 column 1 to the last piece, row 2 column 1, a Fabric F piece.

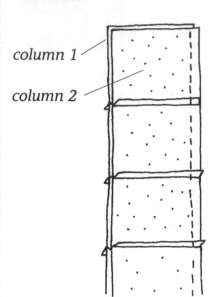

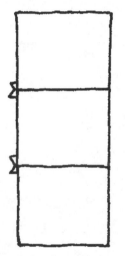

Continue adding squares until you complete the column. Do the same for all of the columns.

Lay out the pieced column strips in their proper order near your ironing board. Press the seam allowances of the first column up toward the top. Press the seam allowances of the second column down. Continue until you have pressed the seam allowances of all the columns. Alternating the direction of the seam allowances will reduce bulk in the finished quilt top.

3. Right sides facing, stitch the column 1 strip to the column 2 strip, matching the seams.

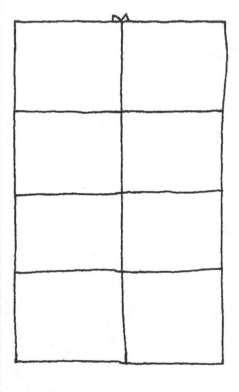

Repeat with column three and so on until you have pieced together all of the strips. Press seams to one side.

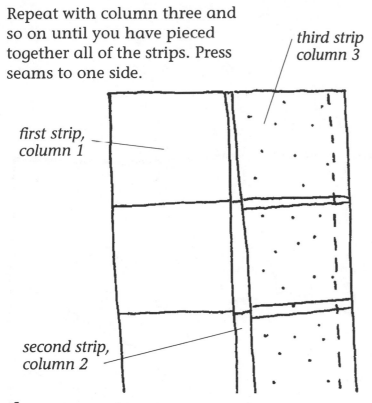

third strip, column 3

first strip, column 1

second strip, column 2

4. Cut the border fabric into 6¹/₂"-wide strips. Stitch to the sides of the quilt top, leaving plenty of extra border fabric at each corner to allow for mitering. Stop and start the stitching ¹/₄" from the corners of the quilt top. Press the seam allowances toward the quilt top.

> ¹/₄"

> ¹/₄"

To miter the corners, fold the quilt right sides together to line up adjacent border strips. Align the miter template with the raw edges of the border. The angled edge of the miter template should intersect the end of the stitching where you stopped stitching the border to the quilt top, ¹/₄" from the edge of the quilt top.

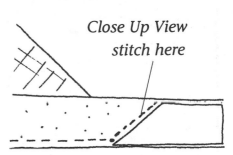

Close Up View stitch here

Mark this line. Stitch. Trim away excess fabric. Press. Press the quilt top.

5. Mark the quilt top for quilting. I have included a diagram of my simple quilt design for reference, or stitch in the ditch along the seam lines.

6. Cut the backing fabric into two 1$\frac{1}{3}$ yard pieces. Trim away the selvedge edges. Seam them together, right sides facing, along one selvedge edge.

Press the seam to one side.

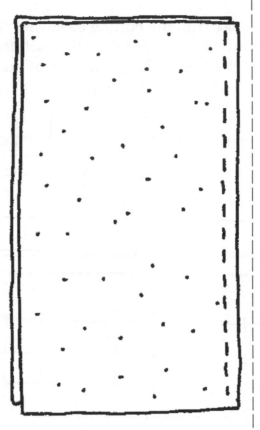

backing wrong side up

7. Lay the backing wrong side up on a flat surface. Smooth it carefully without stretching it. Lay the batting on top. Lay the quilt top right side up on top. Make sure there is excess backing and batting all the way around the quilt top. Use safety pins every 5" or so to baste the quilt sandwich together.

Quilt by hand or machine.

quilt top right side up

batting

8. Trim the batting even with the quilt top. Trim the backing to 1" larger than the quilt top. Fold the backing ¹/2" to the inside along one edge of the quilt top. Fold it ¹/2" to the front of the quilt top. Pin.

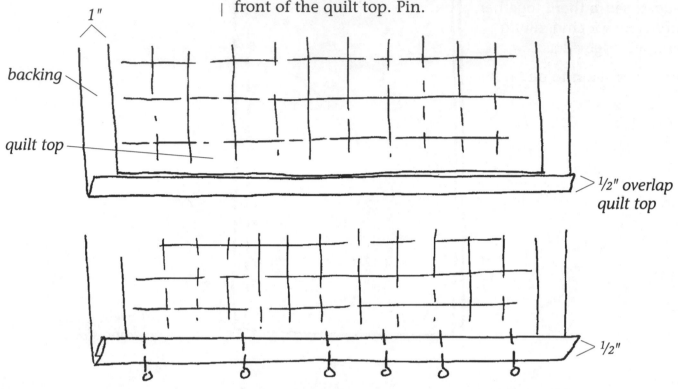

1"

backing

quilt top

> ¹/2" overlap
quilt top

> ¹/2"

Continue around all four sides. Hand or machine stitch to bind the quilt.

9. To make a sleeve for hanging the quilt, cut a 44" x 6" piece of fabric. Press the short edges ¹/4" to the wrong side. Repeat. Topstitch.

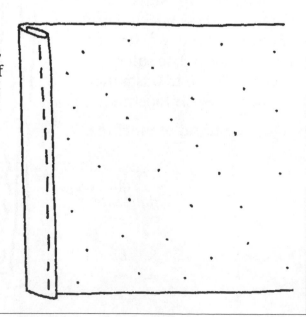

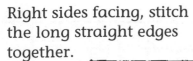

Right sides facing, stitch the long straight edges together.

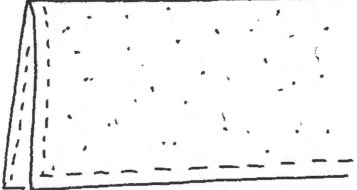

Press the seam allowances open. Turn the sleeve right side out. Press so the seam is at about the center of what will be the back of the sleeve.

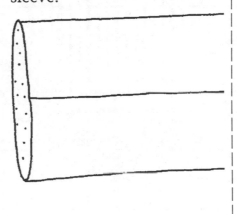

Hand stitch the top and bottom edges of the sleeve to the back of the quilt as shown.

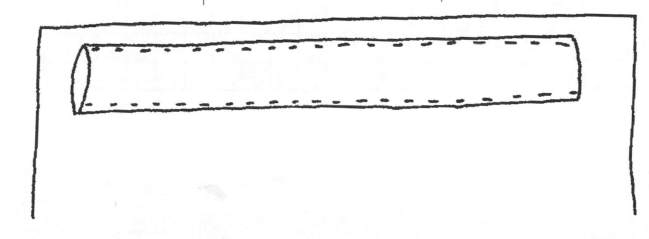

Quilt Piecing Diagram

Fabric Key to Quilt Piecing Diagram

SYMBOL	FABRIC	COLOR OF SQUARES
	A	background
	B	dark red/pink heart
	C	medium/dark red/pink heart
	D	medium red/pink heart
	E	light red/pink heart
	F	green leaves
	G	yellow flower centers
	H	purple flowers

Miter Template

"STAINED GLASS" THROW PILLOWS

Finished pillow size is 16" x 16".

These pretty pillows, made with a stained glass design, are a scrap hoarder's dream! Wonder-Under™ and machine bias applique techniques make this an easy project for all crafters. I used a blue square applique base, then fused the colored "stained glass" pieces to it.

The bias strips for the "lead" in the stained glass are simply made using bias pressing bars. They are available at quilt shops, some fabric stores, and the mail order sources at the end of the book.

26

MATERIALS

For each pillow:

1½ yards black cotton fabric for backing and bias "lead"

½ yard blue fabric for applique quilt top base

Matching thread

Scraps of jewel-colored fabrics (purple, yellow, jade, green...)

One 16" x 16" pillow form

2¼ yards black piping

¾ yard Wonder-Under™

INSTRUCTIONS

Note: All seam allowances are ¼" unless otherwise specified.

Prewash and iron your fabrics.

For the pillow top applique base (blue), cut one square approximately 18" x 18". You will be placing the colored "glass" pieces over the pillow top applique base. The blue pieces will actually be the applique base showing through. For the pillow back, cut two rectangles from the black fabric, each 10½" x 16½".

Bias strips are used for the leading in the pillows. Bias strips are easy to make with the help of bias bars. These handy, flat metal or plastic bars are slipped inside a strip of bias that has been sewn along its long, raw edges. With the bar inside, the strip is pressed so that the seam allowances are hidden at the back of the strip.

Refer to the bias bars package to determine the correct size for cutting your bias strips.

Wrong sides facing, stitch long edges together.

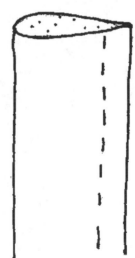

Using bias bar, press so seam is hidden at back.

Make approximately 10 yards of ³⁄₈"-wide bias strips for each pillow.

1. Lay the "stained glass" pattern pieces on the Wonder-Under™ leaving ¹/₂" or so between them. Trace around the pattern pieces and mark them with the color indicated on the pattern. You may substitute whatever color fabrics you desire. The color labels are there only as a key.

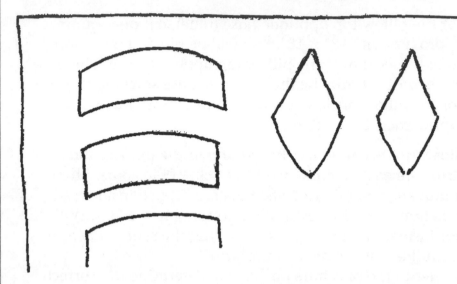

Cut out the pieces outside the traced lines.

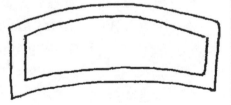

Fuse the pieces with the Wonder-Under™ to the respective fabrics according to the manufacturer's instructions. Cut along the traced lines.

2. Tape the stained glass quilt top pattern to a window. Tape the blue pillow top on top. Using a pencil, trace the design lines as well as the lines indicating the outside square onto the blue fabric.

3. Place the pillow top, marked side up, on your ironing surface. Peel the paper backing off the Wonder-Under™. Arrange the "stained glass" pieces in their proper places on the pillow top. Fuse as instructed on the Wonder-Under™.

4. Following the numbers in the leading order diagram; position the black lead so it is centered over the raw edges of the shapes. Machine stitch first one side and then the other of each piece of bias in place.

bias

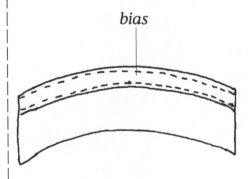

5. Pin and stitch the piping to the right side of the pillow top. Leave 3" to 4" or so of extra piping at the beginning and end of the stitching. At the corners of the pillow, clip the seam allowances of the piping as shown.

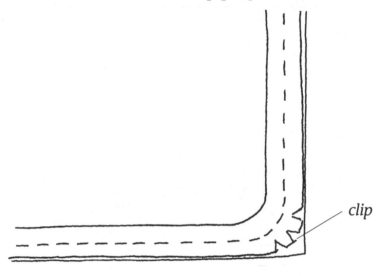

clip

rope

clip

Join the ends of the piping neatly.

trim to 1/2"

fold under 1/4" and baste

6. Press under 1/4" on one long edge of each black pillow back piece. Repeat. Topstitch. Right sides facing, pin the three remaining raw edges of the backing pieces to the pillow top. Stitch.

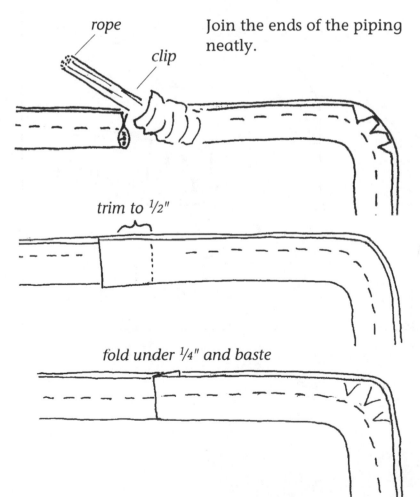

first black pillow back piece

pillow top

first black pillow back piece

second black pillow back piece

pillow top

7. Trim the corners. Turn right side out. Insert the pillow form into the pillow cover.

Color Diagram Enlarge pattern 400% and make 2 copies.
To make glass pattern pieces, cut shapes out
along design lines of one copy of the pattern.

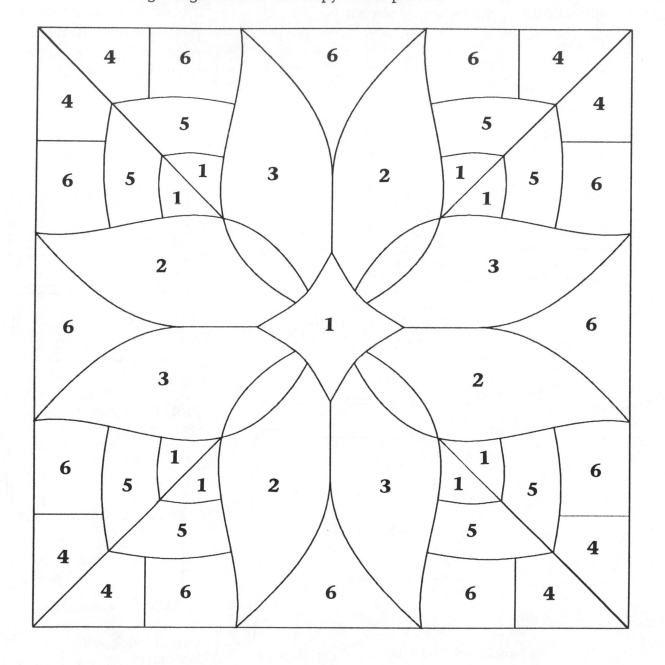

1 = yellow
2 = bright purple
3 = medium purple
4 = dark purple
5 = green
6 = blue

Leading Diagram Stitch all #1's first, then #2's, etc., so that bias strips overlap raw edges of previously stitched pieces.

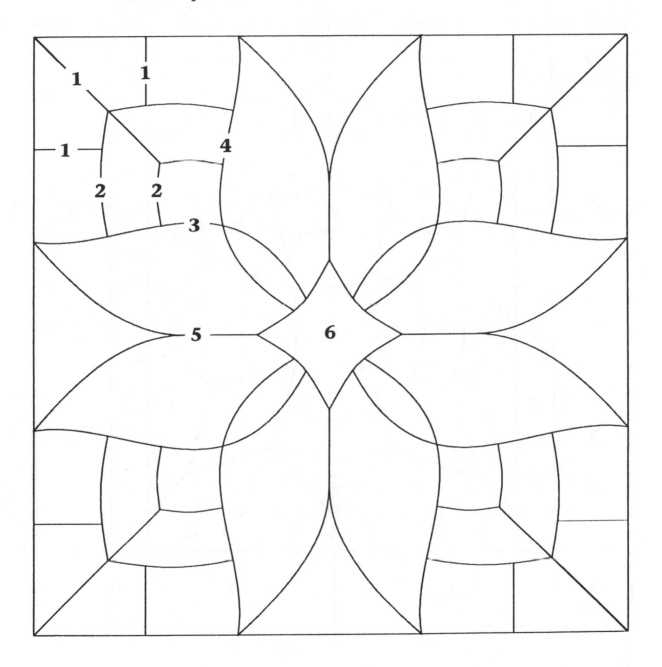

Color Diagram Enlarge pattern 400% and make 2 copies. To make glass pattern pieces, cut shapes out along design lines of one copy of the pattern.

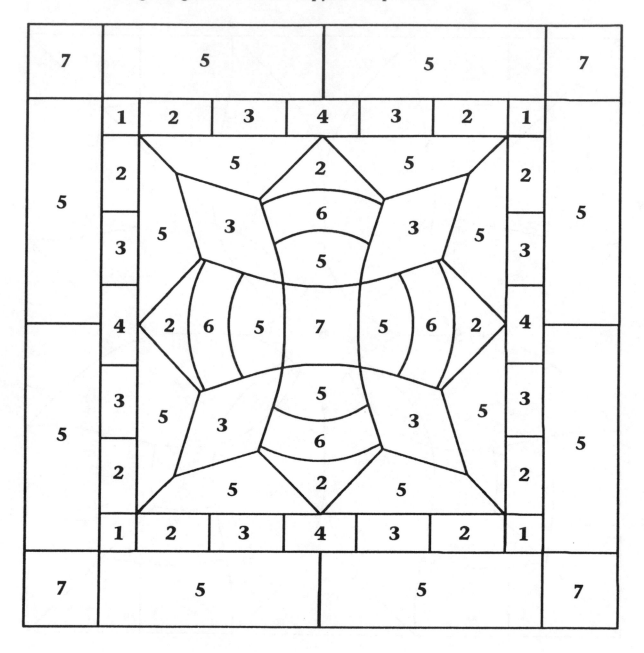

1 = red
2 = green
3 = gold
4 = medium purple
5 = blue
6 = dark purple
7 = bright purple

Leading Diagram Stitch all #1's first, then #2's, etc., so that bias strips overlap raw edges of previously stitched pieces.

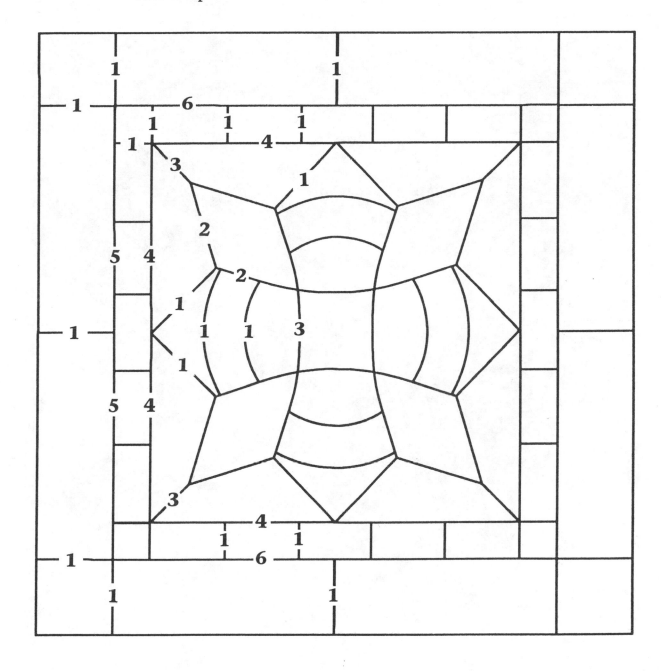

APPLIQUED TABLECLOTH

Finished size 52" square.

Dress up your dining room table with this beautiful appliqued cloth. The applique motif is derived from the feather quilting designs cherished by generations of quilters.

MATERIALS

1½ yards 54" or wider fabric for tablecloth

1⅝ yards fabric for appliques

Matching thread (I used eight 110 yard spools)

3 yards tear-away stabilizer

INSTRUCTIONS

1. Prewash all fabrics.

2. Cut the tablecloth fabric into a 52" square.

Stitch ½" from the edge all the way around. To fray, pull threads from each edge.

3. Lay the stabilizer over the applique pattern. Trace. Repeat seven times to make a total of seven tracings of the feather pattern. Cut them out, an inch or so outside of the traced lines.

Working along one edge of the tablecloth, pin one piece of the stabilizer to the wrong side of the table-cloth, positioning it as shown.

Pin a second piece of stabi-lizer in place, overlapping the leading end of the second piece over the base end of the first piece.

4. Baste along the marked lines of the feather pattern. Disregard the parts of the first piece that are under the second piece.

Trim the applique fabric to the basting, so that it remains just in the feather shapes. Trim the fabric to the inside of the stitching between the basted stem lines (see pattern).

5. From the right side of the tablecloth, satin stitch over the basting.

6. Tear the stabilizer from the back of the tablecloth.

marked stabilizer

Do the same for all four edges of the tablecloth. Cut a piece of applique fabric to fit generously over each feather applique. Pin wrong side of applique fabric to right side of tablecloth.

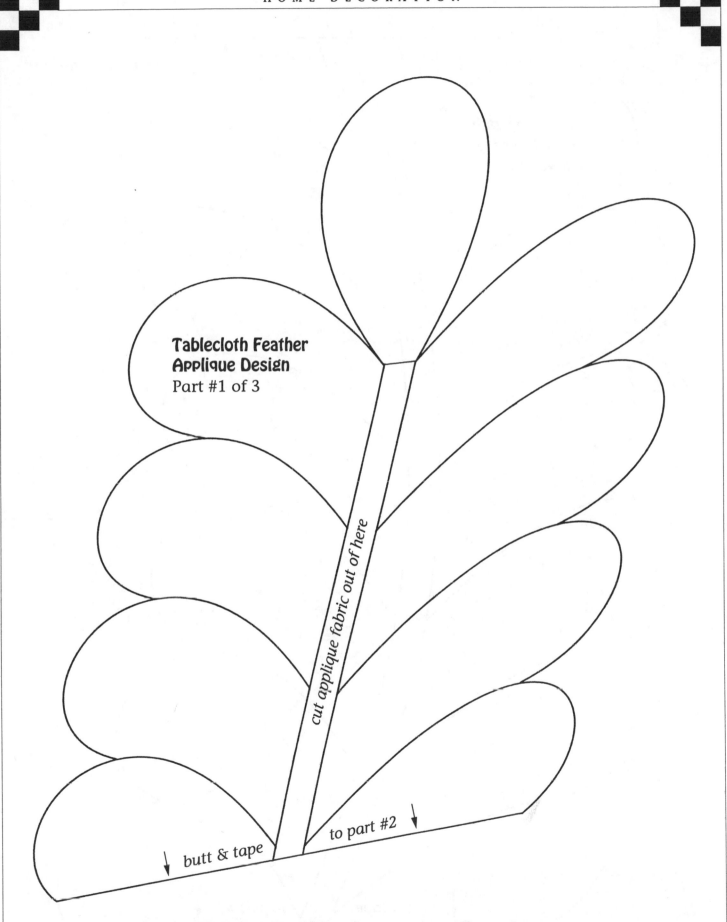

**Tablecloth Feather
Applique Design**
Part #1 of 3

cut applique fabric out of here

butt & tape

to part #2

↑ butt & tape   to part #1 ↑

Tablecloth Feather
Applique Design
Part #2 of 3

↓ butt & tape   to part #3 ↓

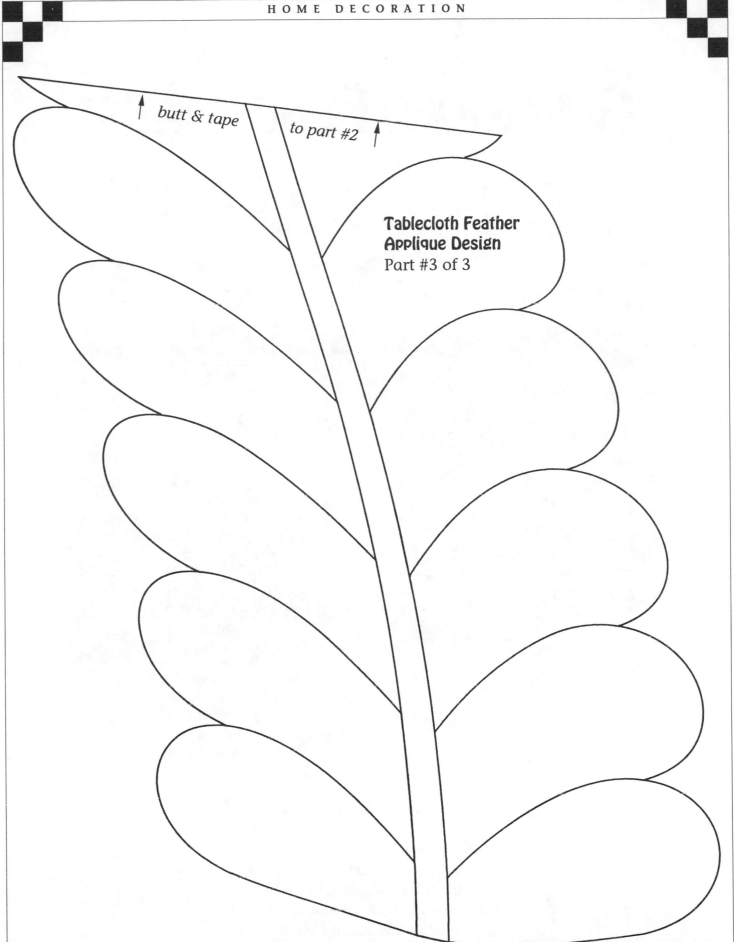

butt & tape

to part #2

**Tablecloth Feather
Applique Design**
Part #3 of 3

APPLIQUED PLACEMATS

Finished size 13" x 18".

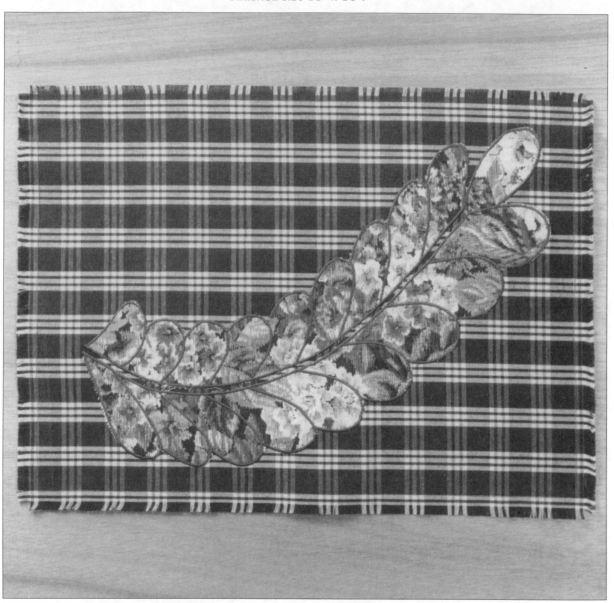

Serve meals in style with these easy-to-make placemats. The feather design is derived from those traditionally used in quilting. The feathers are appliqued to the placemats with a machine satin stitch, and the edges are simply frayed.

MATERIALS

³/₈ yard fabric for two placemats; ⁷/₈ yard for four

Large scraps of fabric for feather applique, or ²/₃ yard fabric

Matching thread

1 yard tear away stabilizer

INSTRUCTIONS

1. Prewash all fabrics.

2. For each placemat cut a 13" x 18" rectangle from the placemat fabric.

Stitch ¹/₂" from the edge all the way around. To fray each edge, pull threads.

3. Lay the stabilizer over the applique pattern. Trace. Pin the stabilizer to the wrong side of the placemat. Cut a piece of applique fabric to fit generously over feather applique. Pin, wrong side of applique fabric toward the right side of placemat. Baste along the marked lines of the feather pattern. Trim the extra fabric away from outside of the basting around the feathers and between the two basted stem lines.

From the right side of the placemat, satin stitch over the basting.

4. Tear the stabilizer away from the back of the placemat.

stitch ¹/₂" from raw edge

To fray, pull threads away from edges.

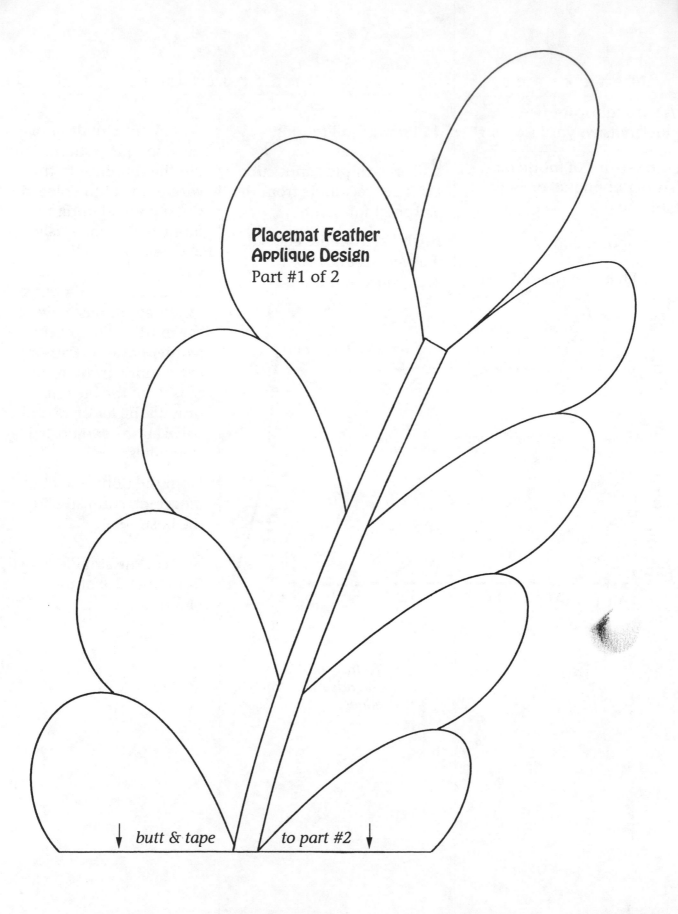

**Placemat Feather
Applique Design**
Part #1 of 2

↓ *butt & tape* *to part #2* ↓

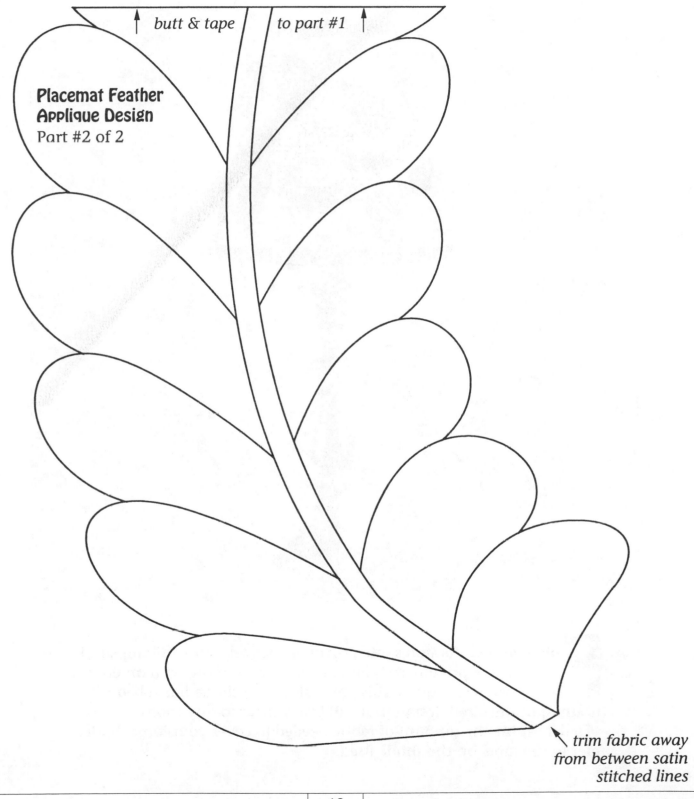

butt & tape   to part #1

Placemat Feather Applique Design
Part #2 of 2

trim fabric away from between satin stitched lines

SCRAP APPLIQUE LAMPSHADE

Fabric and crafts stores often carry attractively shaped lampshade lines. These pre-glued shades are easy to decorate with an endless variety of techniques. This particular lampshade has a beautiful album quilt-inspired design that will bring cheer to any room.

To determine the amount of fabric needed to cover your lampshade, refer to the label on the shade itself.

MATERIALS

One pre-glued lampshade

Fabric scraps

Fabric to cover lampshade
(see above)

One package extra wide,
double-fold bias tape

White glue

Wonder-Under™

INSTRUCTIONS

Prepare all patterns as instructed on page 10.

1. Trace the applique designs onto the paper backing of the Wonder-Under™. Space them 1/2" or more apart. The number of applique pieces needed will vary depending upon the size of the shade and the way you place them. For a 4" x 8" x 7" shade, I use three flowers, three stem pieces, five buds, and eleven leaves. Generally, it is a good idea to make more than you expect to need.

2. Cut out the applique shapes, 1/4" or so outside of the traced lines.

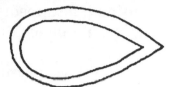

Following the manufacturer's instructions, fuse the Wonder-Under™ to the wrong sides of the appropriate fabrics.

3. Cut the appliques out on the traced lines. To avoid fraying the cut edges of the appliques, handle them as little as possible once cut.

To remove the paper backing from the appliques, make a tear in the paper with the tip of your scissors. This will give you a hold on the paper to tear it away.

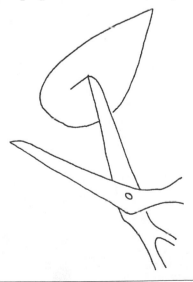

4. Remove the paper covering the lampshade. Use it as a pattern for cutting out the shade covering fabric. Cut the fabric about 1" larger all around than the pattern. Trace the pattern onto the fabric using a disappearing marker or light pencil lines.

5. Lay the shade covering fabric right side up on your ironing board. Arrange the applique pieces on top, using your marked lines as a guide for the boundaries of the shade. Following the Wonder-Under™ instructions, fuse the appliques to the fabric.

6. Following the manufacturer's instructions, apply the fabric to the lampshade. Trim the fabric at the seam to overlap 1/2" or so.

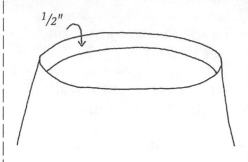

1/2" overlap

7. Trim the excess fabric at the top and bottom of the shade to 3/8". Fold to the inside of the lampshade and glue in place.

1/2"

8. Glue the bias tape to the top and bottom of the shade. Fold the second end under to hide the raw edge.

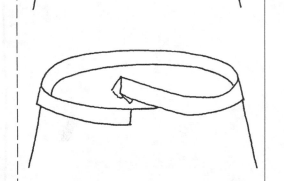

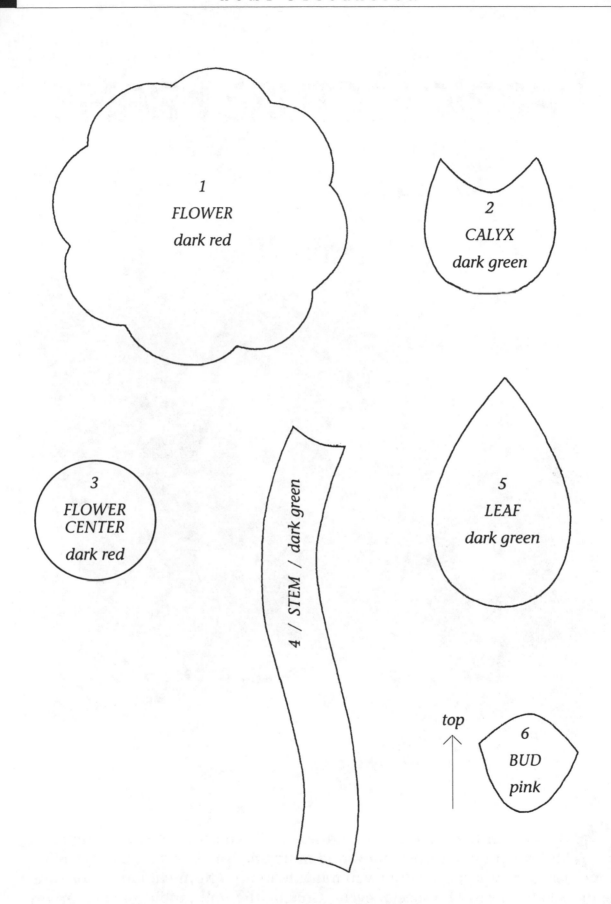

1
FLOWER
dark red

2
CALYX
dark green

3
FLOWER
CENTER
dark red

4 / STEM / dark green

5
LEAF
dark green

top

6
BUD
pink

FABRIC PICTURE FRAME

Finished size: Large 8½" x 10½" • Small 5½" x 7½"

Display your treasured photos in these easily constructed fabric frames. Make a gift of a throw pillow and matching frame or two. Or, use a scrap from a special dress you made to make a frame holding a picture of the dress being worn at a special event. Gracing the walls, table, or shelf in any room, these frames will bring you and your family or friends years of pleasure.

 MATERIALS

Four pieces of fabric, each 9$^{1}/_{2}$" x 11$^{1}/_{2}$" for large frame, or 6$^{1}/_{2}$" x 8$^{1}/_{2}$" for small frame

Matching thread

Batting scrap

Cardboard: 8" x 10" for large frame, 5" x 7" for small frame

One metal ring for hanging

INSTRUCTIONS

Note: All seam allowances are ¼" unless otherwise specified.

Prepare all patterns as instructed on page 10.

1. Lay the frame pattern on the wrong side of one of the rectangles. Trace the window onto the fabric.

2. Cut a piece of batting the same size as the rectangles.

3. Lay an unmarked rectangle, right side up, on top of the batting. Lay the marked rectangle on top, right side down. Stitch along the marked line for the window, through all layers. Trim the inside oval away, leaving a $^{1}/_{8}$" seam allowance.

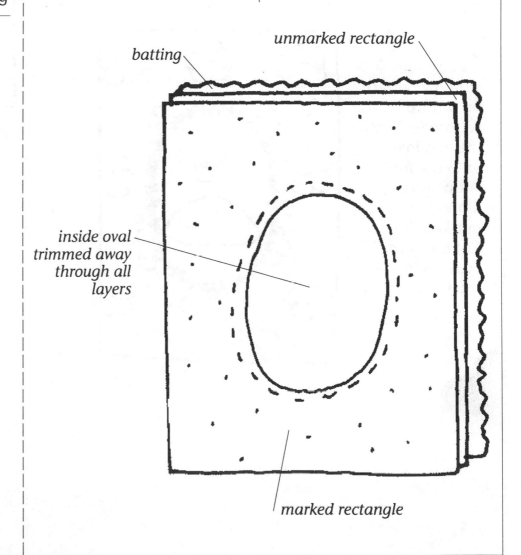

batting

unmarked rectangle

inside oval trimmed away through all layers

marked rectangle

Turn right sides out. Press. Baste the outside edges together through all three layers.

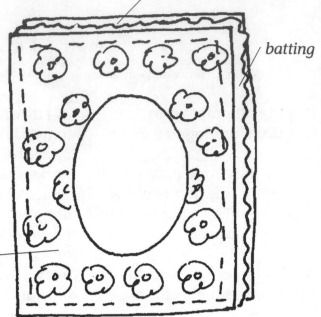

unmarked rectangle

batting

marked rectangle

4. Lay the window pattern on a third rectangle. Trace the window onto the fabric. Satin stitch along the marked line. Cut away the oval inside the stitching.

5. Press ¼" to the wrong side on one short edge of the remaining rectangle. Repeat. Topstitch. This is the back of the frame.

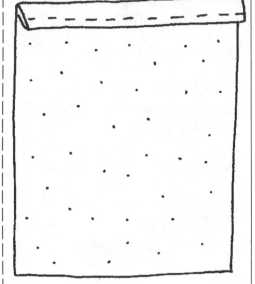

6. Lay the window piece, wrong side up, on your work surface. Lay the back frame piece on top, right side up. Have the unfinished edges match the raw edges of the fabric beneath.

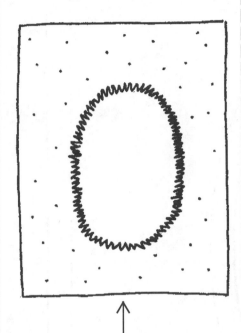

Lay the padded frame on top, wrong side up.

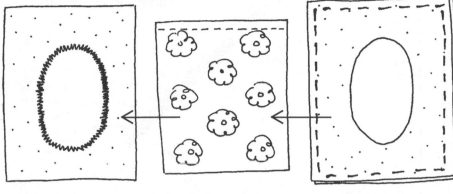

window piece   *back frame piece*   *padded frame*

Match and pin all edges. Stitch all the way around.

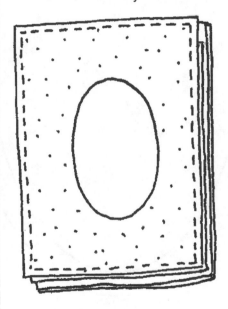

Trim corners. Turn right side out.

7. Insert the cardboard between the back and the window. Put the photo in front of the cardboard.

8. Stitch the metal ring to the center back of the frame.

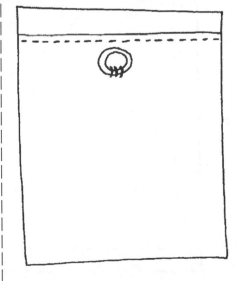

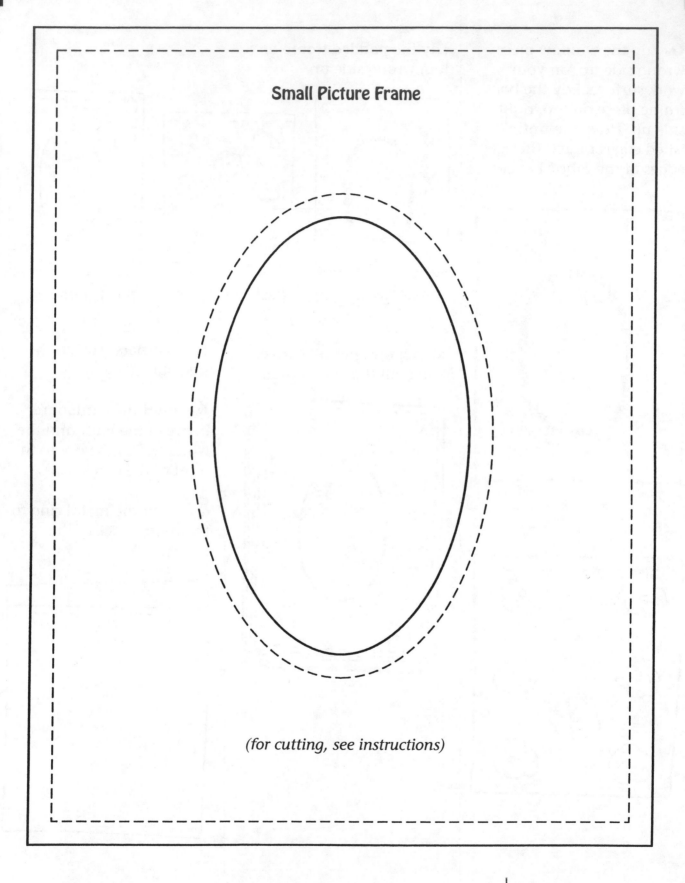

Small Picture Frame

(for cutting, see instructions)

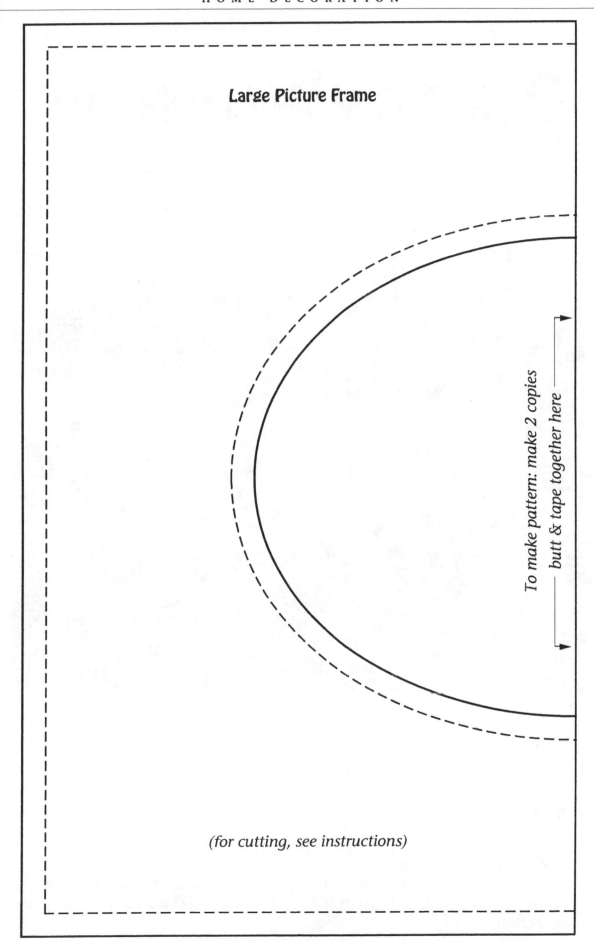

Large Picture Frame

To make pattern: make 2 copies
— butt & tape together here →

(for cutting, see instructions)

QUILTED WALLHANGING

Finished size is 30" long x 40" wide.

This wallhanging, with a decorative tulip design, uses rotary cutting techniques and quick piecing to turn scrap fabrics into a quilted spring flower garden.

Included are yardages for the fabrics, should you wish to purchase new fabrics for the quilts. Or, use this as a guide for selecting scraps from your collection.

MATERIALS

¹/₄ yard fabric A

¹/₄ yard fabric B

³/₈ yard fabric C

³/₈ yard fabric D

¹/₄ yard fabric E

¹/₄ yard fabric F

³/₈ yard border fabric

Matching thread

1 yard backing fabric

Batting

Quilting thread

INSTRUCTIONS

Note: All seam allowances are ¼".

Prewash and iron your fabrics.

1. Cut the fabric into strips according to the following chart:

Fabric Key to Wallhanging Strips

SYMBOL	FABRIC	# OF 2¹/₂"-WIDE STRIPS	# OF 2⁷/₈"-WIDE STRIPS
	A	1	1
	B	1	1
	C	1	1
	D	1	2
	E	2	1
	F	1	1

55

2. Cut the fabrics into squares, strips, and triangles according to the following charts.

Square Cutting Chart: Cut squares from the 2¹/₂"-wide strips.

SYMBOL	FABRIC	# OF SQUARES
	A	3
	B	3
	C	12
	D	18
	E	33
	F	15

To make the triangles, first cut the 2⁷/₈"-wide strips into 2⁷/₈" squares. Then cut them diagonally into triangles according to the chart. Note that each square makes two triangles.

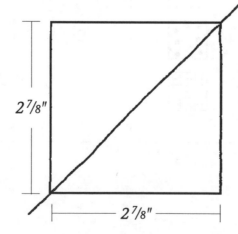

2⁷/₈"

2⁷/₈"

Triangle Cutting Chart:

FABRIC		# OF TRIANGLES
A		24
B		24
C		18
D		42
E		12
F		12

3. Right sides facing, stitch the triangles together along their diagonal (bias) edges according to the following chart:

Triangle Cutting Chart:

FABRICS		# TO PIECE FOR A 3-BLOCK QUILT
AD		12
AB		12
BC		12
CD		6
DE		12
DF		12

For example, piece
one triangle A to one
triangle D.

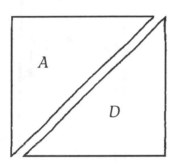

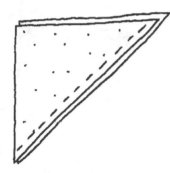

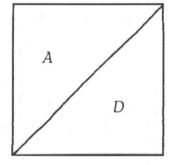

Repeat until you
have twelve triangle
AD pairs. Work down
the chart in this
manner.

Press the seam allow-
ances to one side.

4. Piece each of the
three tulip blocks in
strips following the
block diagram.

Block Diagram

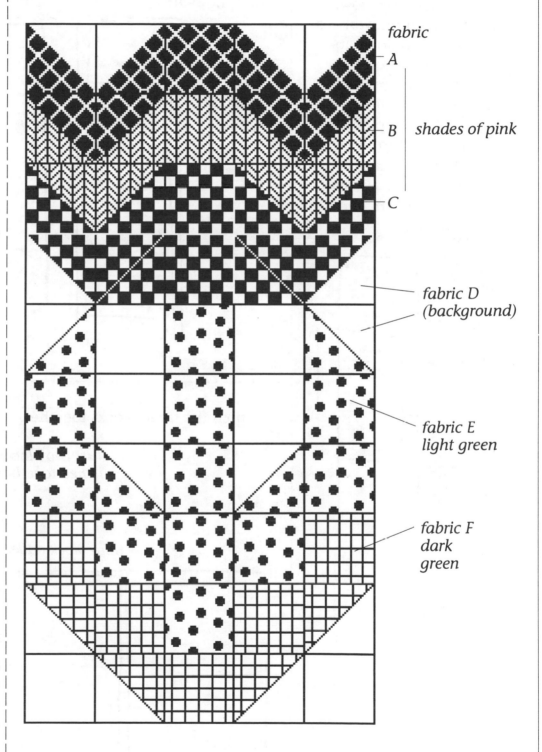

fabric

A

B   *shades of pink*

C

*fabric D
(background)*

*fabric E
light green*

*fabric F
dark
green*

5. Lay the strips for one block in order face down. Press the seam allowances of the first strip down toward the bottom of the strip. For the second strip, press the seam allowances up, toward the top of the strips. For the third, down toward the bottom of the strip, and so forth. Repeat for the strips for the remaining two blocks.

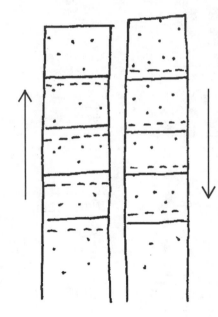

6. Stitch the strips for each block together, carefully matching seams.

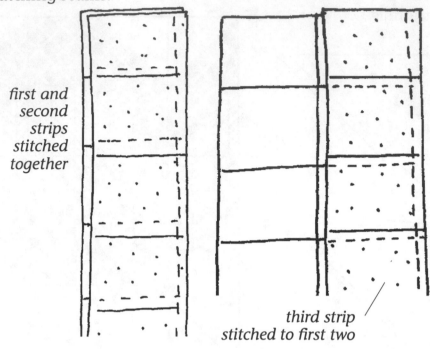

first and second strips stitched together

third strip stitched to first two

7. Stitch the three blocks together.

first two blocks stitched together

third block added

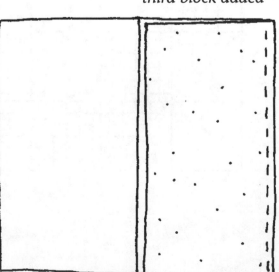

Press all seam allowances to one side.

Quilt Top Diagram

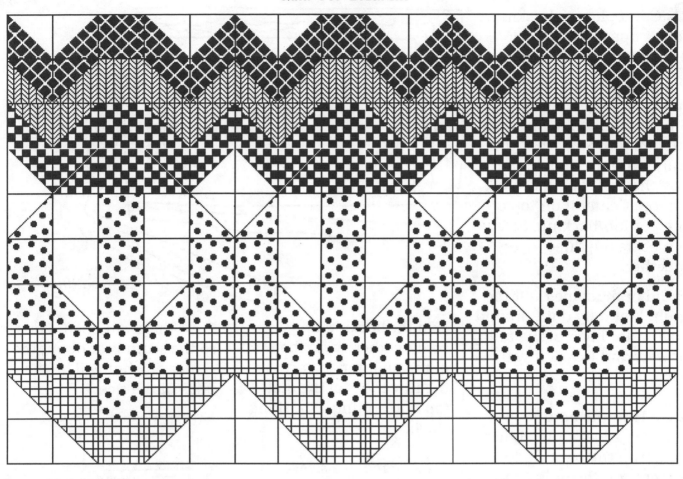

8. For the border, cut four strips, each 6" x 30 1/2".

Stitch two of the strips to the bottom and top edges of the pieced quilt top.

Press the seam allowances toward the border strip.

Stitch the two remaining strips to the side edges of the quilt top.

Press the seam allowances toward the border.

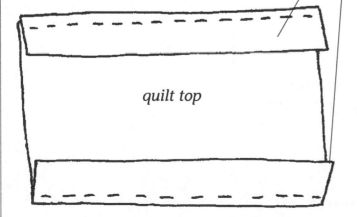

border strips

quilt top

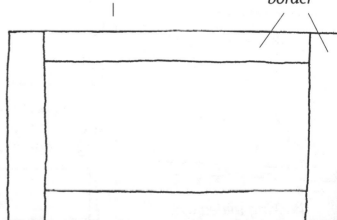

border

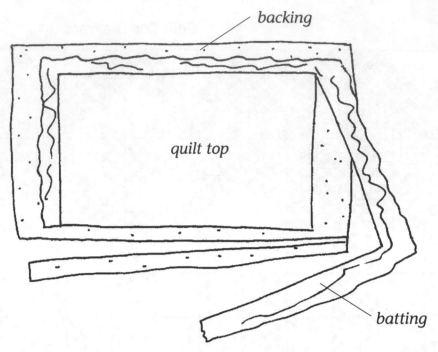

backing

quilt top

batting

9. Cut a piece of backing fabric approximately 36" x 46". Repeat for the batting.

Place the backing right side down on your work surface. Smooth it flat. Lay the batting on top. Smooth it carefully, without stretching it. Lay the quilt top, face up, on top. Center it on top of the batting/backing. Safety pin baste the three layers together.

Hand or machine quilt the quilt. You may quilt around each color layer of the tulip flowers and leaves if you wish.

10. Trim the batting even with the edge of the quilt top. Trim the backing to 1" larger than the quilt top.

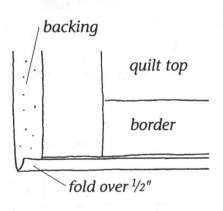

backing

quilt top

border

fold over 1/2"

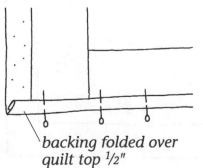

backing folded over quilt top 1/2"

Fold the backing up 1/2". Fold another 1/2" to the front of the quilt top to encase the raw edges of the quilt top and batting. Pin. Hand stitch.

11. To make a sleeve for hanging the quilt, cut a 36" x 6" piece of fabric. Press the short edges 1/4" to the wrong side. Repeat. Topstitch.

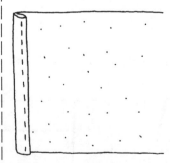

Wrong sides facing, fold and stitch the long straight edges together.

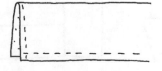

Press the seam open. Press so the seam is at about the center of what will be the back of the sleeve.

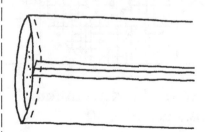

Hand stitch to the back of the quilt as shown.

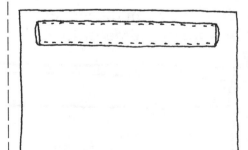

FOLK ART
· SOFT ·
SCULPTURE

FOLK ART TIGER CAT

Finished size is 16" tall.

Nestled among the pillows on your sofa or chair, this folk art tiger cat will invite visitors to sit a while.

The cat is made from two layers of fabric. The base fabric is cut to size, then the fabric used to make the cat's stripes is appliqued on top, using a machine satin stitch. (I used a light fabric for the base and a darker fabric for the stripes.) The back of the cat is also made from the fabric used for the stripes.

The eyes, nose, and mouth are appliqued.

To make a bendable tail, use a length of foam-covered wire, the type used for tying tomatoes to their stakes. Three pipe cleaners wound together lengthwise also work well.

MATERIALS

1/3 yard fabric for the body (under the stripes)

1/2 yard fabric for the back and the appliqued stripes

Matching thread

1/2 yard stabilizer

Polyester fiberfill stuffing

Scrap of fabric for eyes

Matching thread

Foam-covered wire or pipe cleaners for tail

INSTRUCTIONS

Note: All seam allowances are ¼" unless otherwise specified.

Prewash and iron your fabrics. Prepare all patterns as instructed on page 10.

1. Cut two rectangles of the fabric for stripe and one from the body fabric, each approximately 12" x 18". For the tail, cut two 6" x 17" or so rectangles, one from the body fabric and one from the fabric for stripes.

2. Trace the patterns for the body and tail onto two pieces of stabilizer. To see the pattern through the stabilizer, tape the pattern to a window. Tape the stabilizer on top. Trace the outside seam lines also.

3. Lay one body rectangle used for stripe, wrong side up, on your work surface. Lay the body fabric rectangle, wrong side up, on top. Lay the marked stabilizer on top of both of these, marked side up.

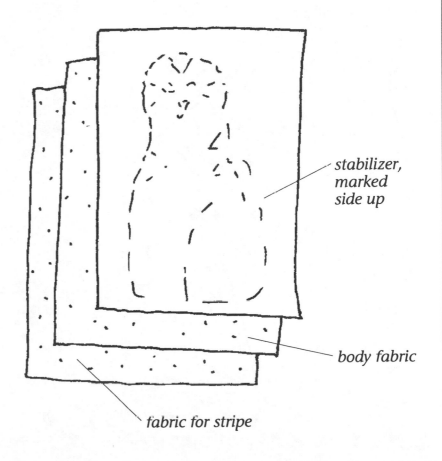

stabilizer, marked side up

body fabric

fabric for stripe

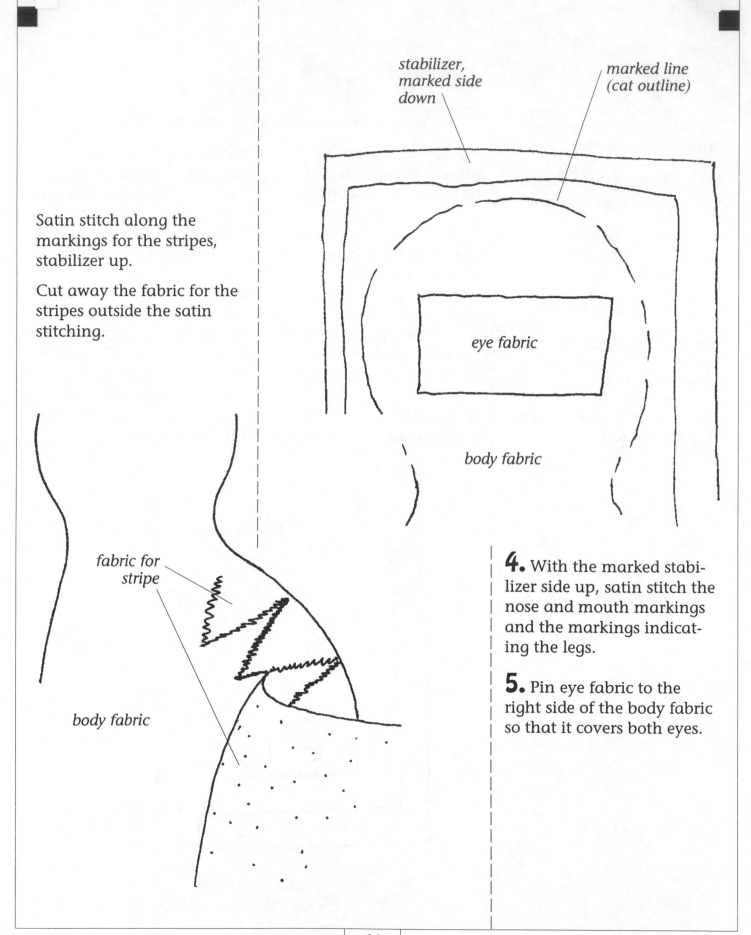

stabilizer, marked side down

marked line (cat outline)

eye fabric

body fabric

Satin stitch along the markings for the stripes, stabilizer up.

Cut away the fabric for the stripes outside the satin stitching.

fabric for stripe

body fabric

4. With the marked stabilizer side up, satin stitch the nose and mouth markings and the markings indicating the legs.

5. Pin eye fabric to the right side of the body fabric so that it covers both eyes.

With stabilizer facing up, satin stitch along the eye markings with matching thread.

Trim the eye fabric to the stitching.

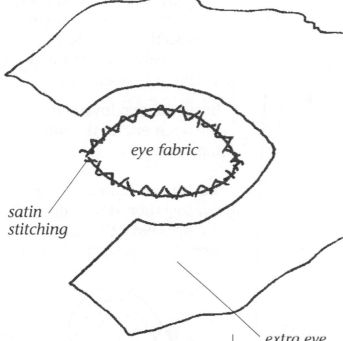

eye fabric

satin stitching

extra eye fabric cut away

From the right side, satin stitch over your previous eye satin stitching.

From the right side, satin stitch the pupils of the eyes. Widen the stitches in the middle.

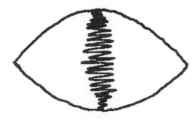

6. For the tail, lay one tail rectangle for stripe, wrong side up, on your work surface. Lay the light fabric rectangle on top, wrong side up. Lay the marked stabilizer on top of both of these, marked side up.

stabilizer

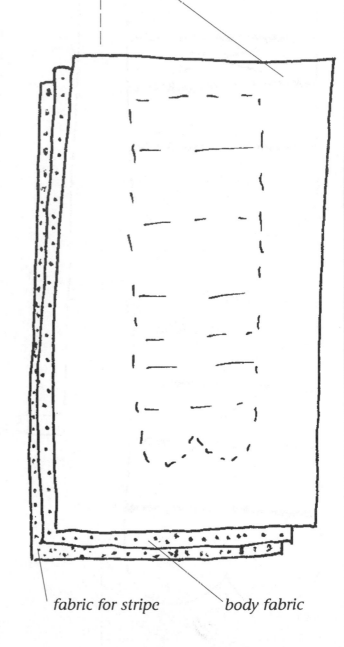

fabric for stripe   *body fabric*

Satin stitch along the markings for stripes, stabilizer up.

Cut away the fabric sections between the satin stitching marked with an x.

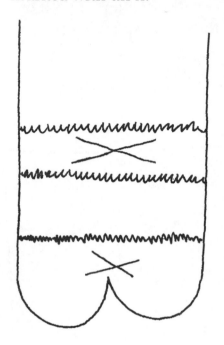

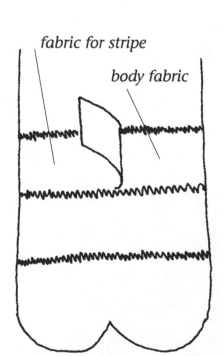

fabric for stripe

body fabric

Fold the tail in half so right sides are together. Stitch along the marked line on the stabilizer, leaving the short straight edge open.

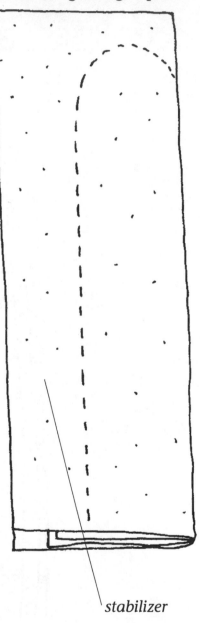

stabilizer

Tear away the stabilizer. Trim the seam allowances to $1/8$".

Turn the tail right side out.

Push a ball of stuffing into the tip of the tail. Insert the foam-covered wire or pipe cleaners, then push stuffing into the tail around them. Stuff softly, so the tail will bend easily. Stuff to about 1" from the open end.

Baste the two layers at the open end of the tail together.

7. Stitch a light and a dark ear together, right sides facing. Leave the short, straight edge open. Repeat.

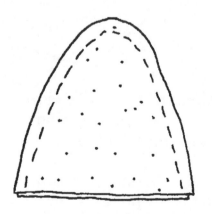

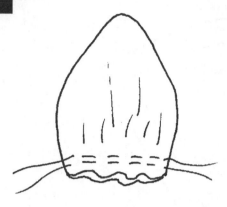

Gather stitch the raw edges together. Pull up on the gather stitches to make the ear about 2½" wide. Pin to the head as shown, light fabric against the front of the head. Baste. Repeat for the other ear.

8. Right side up, lay the remaining fabric for the stripes on your work surface. Right side down, lay the appliqued front of the cat on top. Stitch along the marked seam line, leaving a 4" opening for turning and stuffing. Leave a 2"-long opening for inserting the tail.

9. Insert the tail onto the opening left for it, with the raw ends 1½" above the bottom stitching line. Stitch.

10. Tear the stabilizer from the fabric. Trim the seam allowances to ½".

11. Turn the cat right side out. Stuff. Ladder stitch the opening in the body closed.

clip

tail inserted between two layers

2"

67

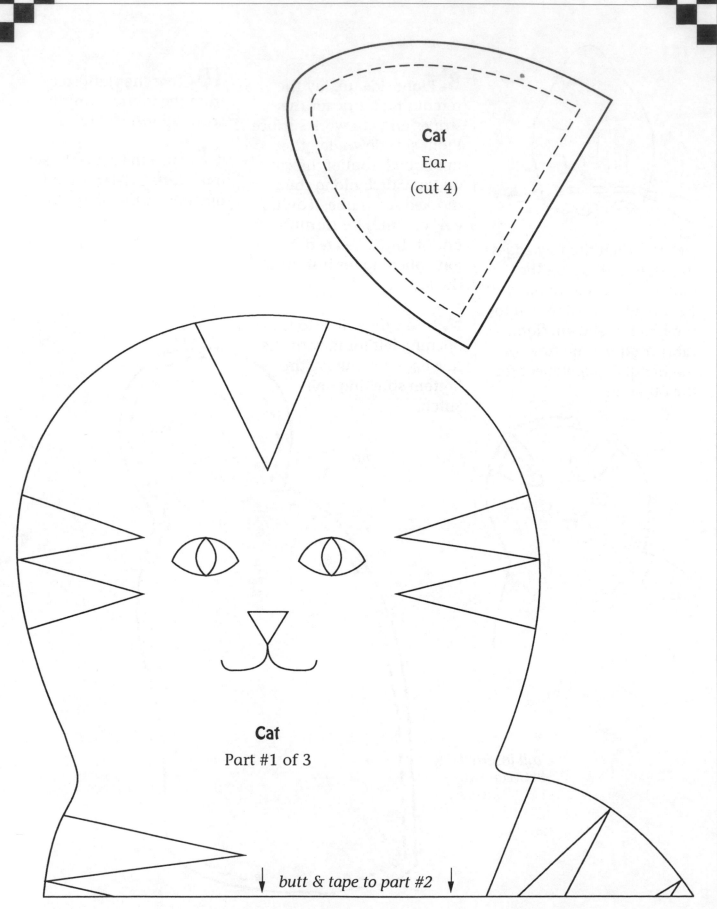

Cat
Ear
(cut 4)

Cat

Part #1 of 3

↓ *butt & tape to part #2* ↓

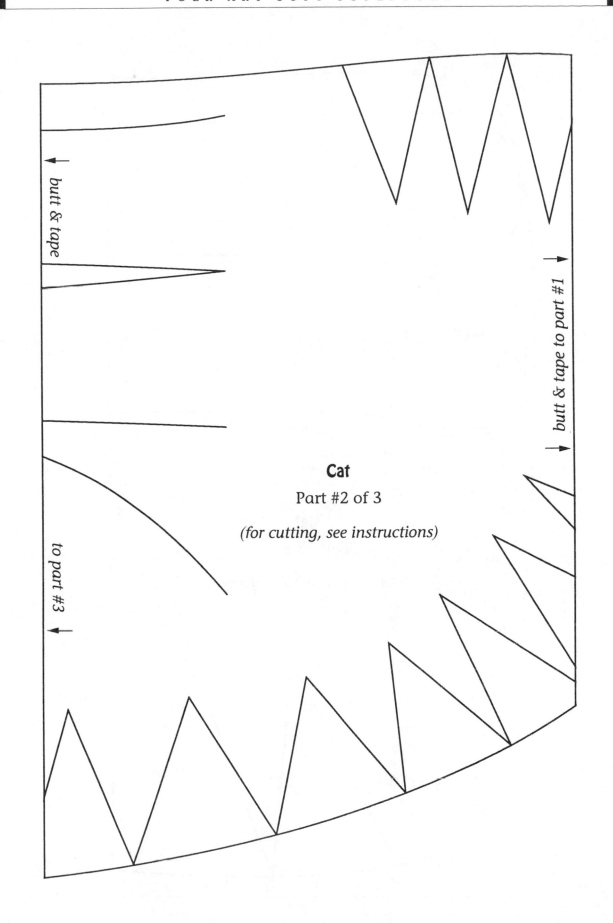

butt & tape

butt & tape to part #1

to part #3

Cat

Part #2 of 3

(for cutting, see instructions)

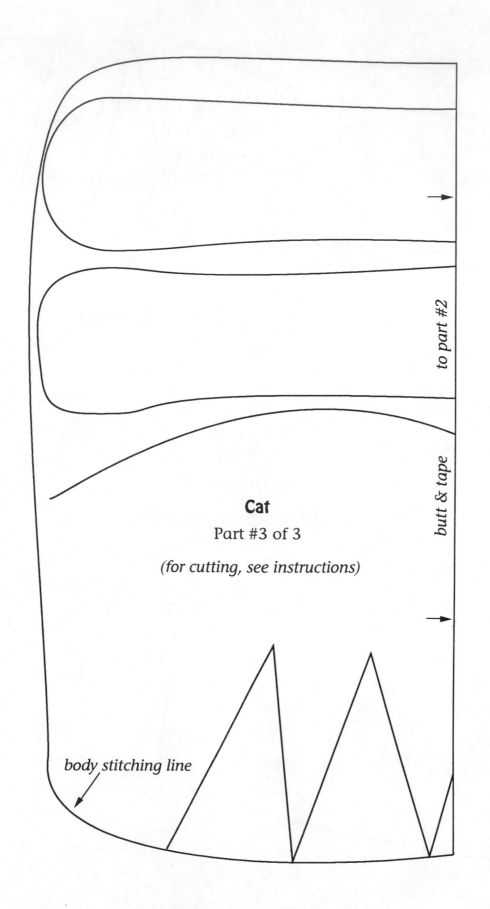

to part #2

butt & tape

Cat

Part #3 of 3

(for cutting, see instructions)

body stitching line

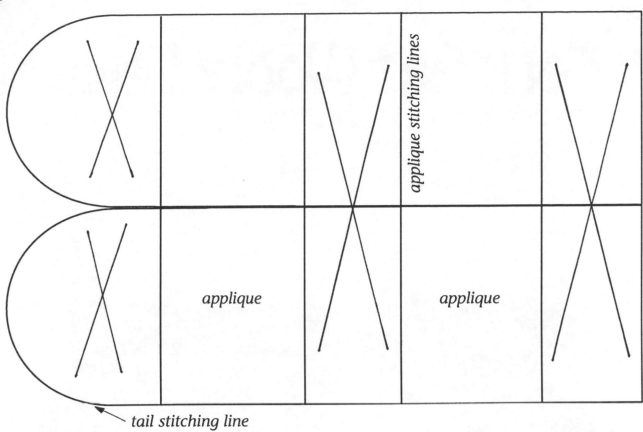

applique stitching lines

applique *applique*

tail stitching line

Cat Tail

*See instructions
before cutting
fabric.*

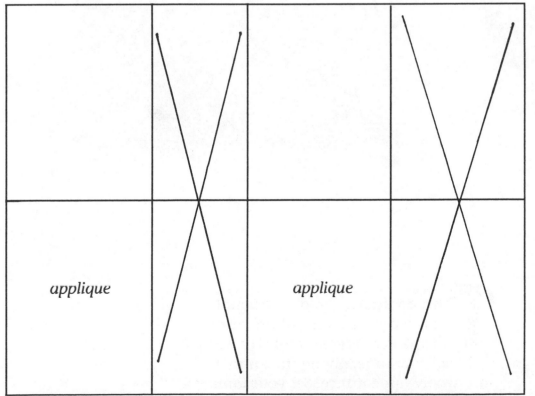

applique *applique*

*Cut out applique from crossed out sections so
base fabric shows through.*

FOLK ART WOOLY LAMB

Finished size is 19" x 11".

This adorable, two-dimensional lamb is covered in cotton fabric strips to resemble wool. The scraps will fray over time, giving the lamb a soft, wooly appearance. Set your lamb on a rocking chair or in a bookcase for a wonderful decorative touch.

ATERIALS

3/8 yard black calico fabric for body

Matching thread

Scraps of black calico fabrics for ears, tail, and leg contrast

Off-white calico fabrics totalling approximately 3 yards for wool

Matching thread

Polyester fiberfill stuffing

INSTRUCTIONS

Note: All seam allowances are ¼".

Prewash and iron your fabrics. Prepare patterns as instructed on page 10. To give the lamb a scrappy look ,use different black calico fabrics for each ear/tail. The ears and tail are made from the same pattern piece.

1. Lay one body side piece right side up on your work surface. To make a leg or head side of a different fabric (this is optional), cut a piece of the second fabric larger than the leg.

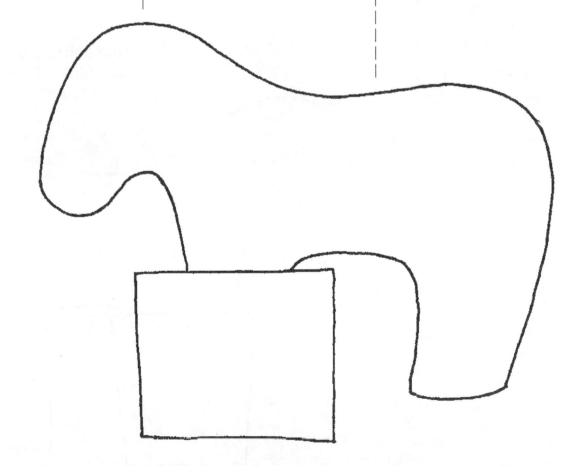

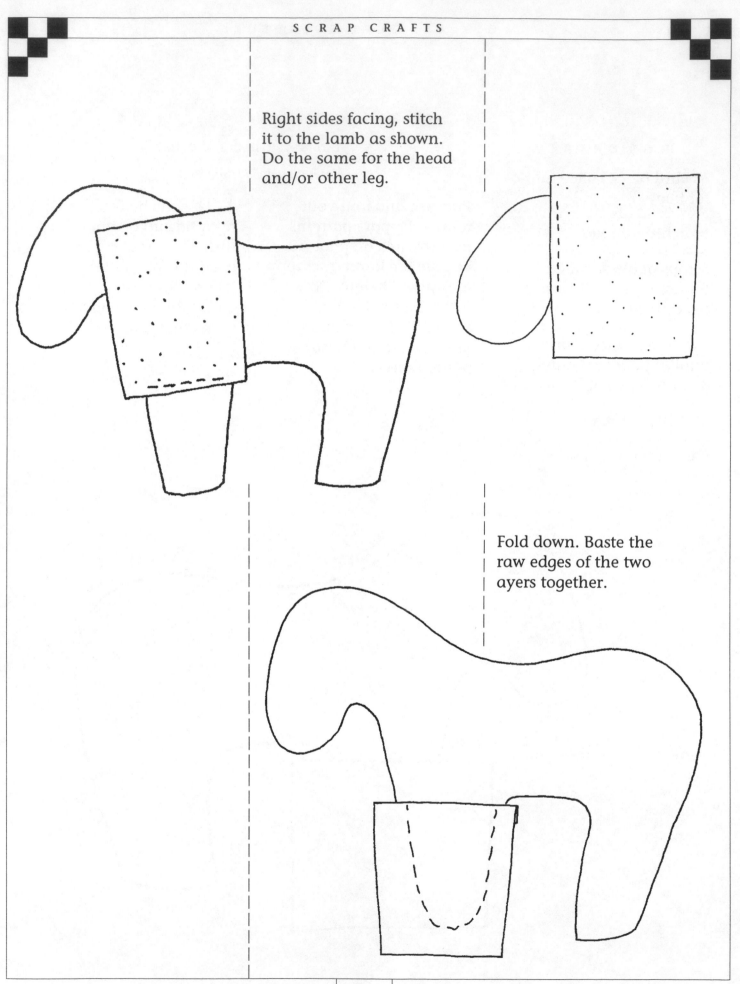

Right sides facing, stitch it to the lamb as shown. Do the same for the head and/or other leg.

Fold down. Baste the raw edges of the two ayers together.

Trim the patched fabric even with the body side it covers.

Repeat for the other body side piece.

2. Right sides facing, stitch the two body pieces together, leaving a 4"-long opening at the bottom for turning and stuffing.

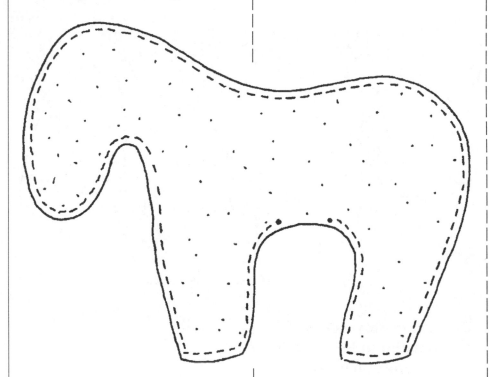

Turn right side out.

3. The ears and tail are made from the same pattern. Right sides facing, pin two ear/tail pieces together. Stitch, leaving the short, straight edges open.

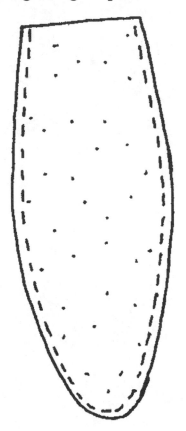

Turn right sides out. Repeat for the remaining two ear/ tails.

4. Starting with the head, stuff the lamb's body. Ladder stitch the opening at the bottom closed.

5. Cut or tear the wool fabric into 1"- to 1¹/₂"-wide strips. A rotary cutter makes quick work of this. Fold in half and stitch to the lamb's body, starting at the head as shown.

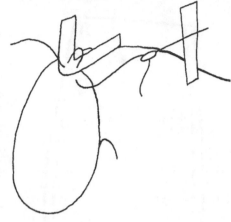

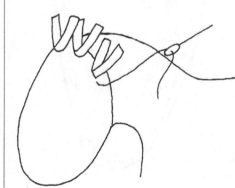

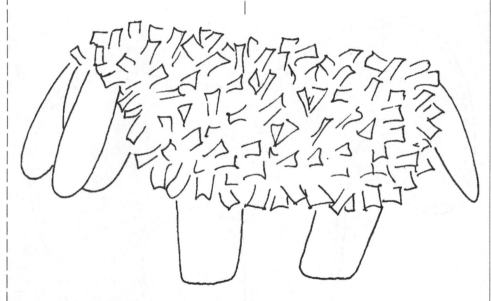

6. Turn the raw edges of the ears and tail ¹/₄" to the inside. Whipstitch closed. Stitch to the lamb.

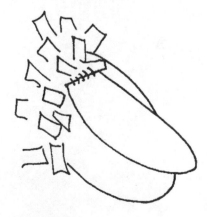

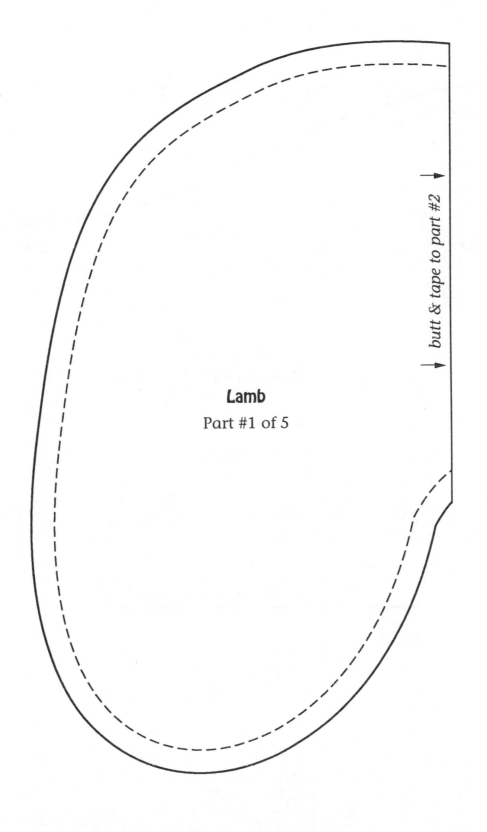

Lamb

Part #1 of 5

butt & tape to part #2

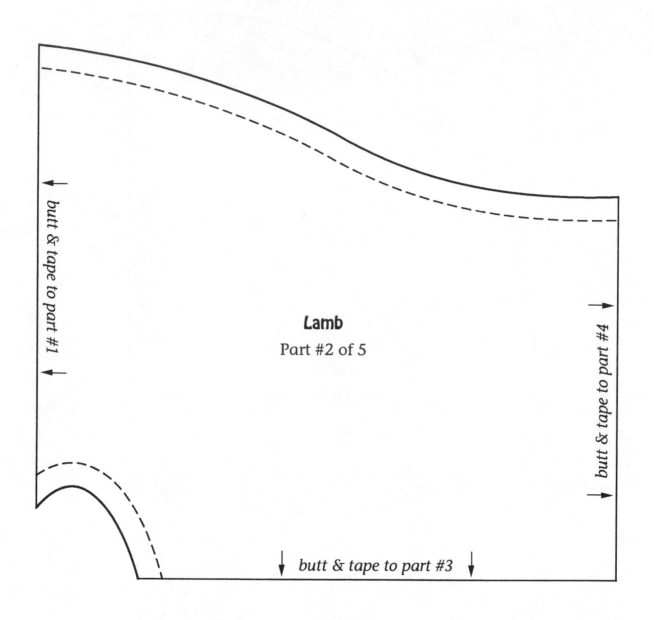

Lamb

Part #2 of 5

butt & tape to part #1

butt & tape to part #4

butt & tape to part #3

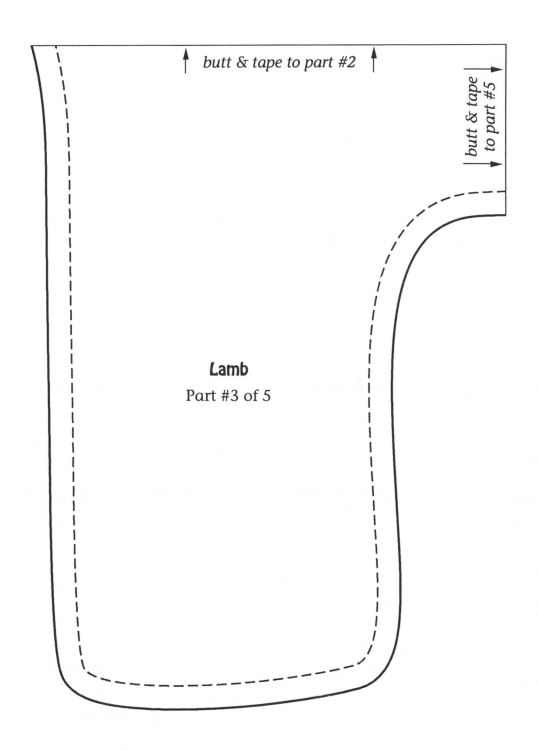

butt & tape to part #2

butt & tape to part #5

Lamb

Part #3 of 5

butt & tape to part #2

Lamb

Part #4 of 5

(cut 2, reverse 1)

 butt & tape to part #5

Lamb

Ear/Tail

(cut 6)

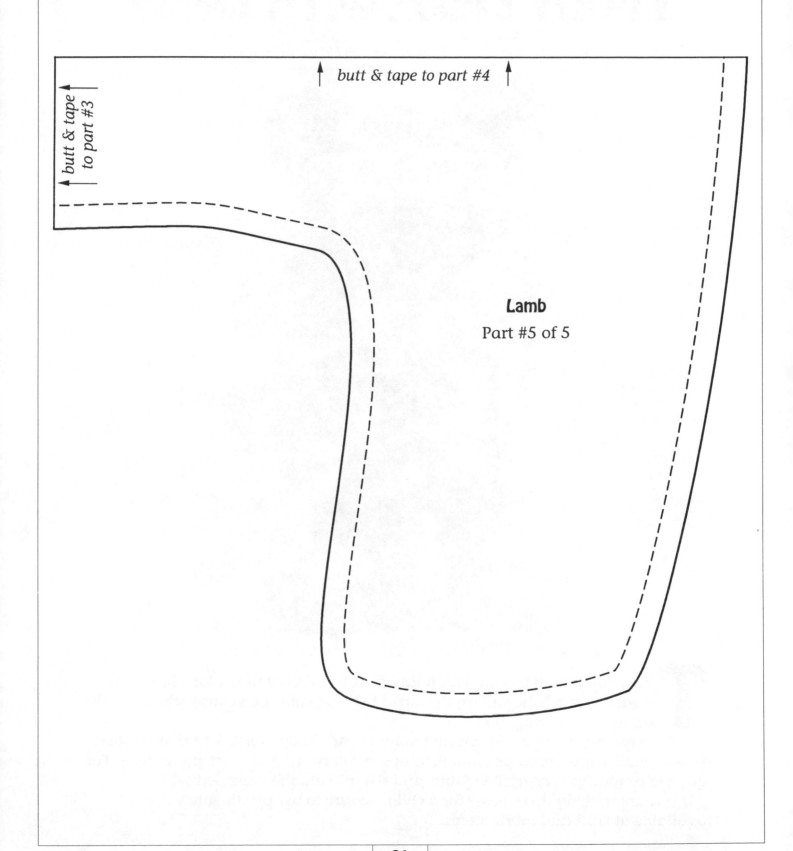

butt & tape to part #4

butt & tape to part #3

Lamb
Part #5 of 5

TEDDY BEAR WITH BABY

Finished size is 16" tall for mama bear, and 9" tall for baby bear.

This scrap-pieced mama bear hugs her baby proudly in her lap. She sits by means of stitch "joints" at the top of her legs, and she's constructed to withstand years of hugging!

There are two methods for piecing mama bear's body fabric. You may choose to use small scraps, or large enough scraps to rotary cut and quick piece strips. For quicker results, use pre-quilted fabric and skip piecing the fabric entirely.

If you are making these bears for a child, be sure to use plastic safety eyes, available at craft and fabric stores.

MATERIALS

Scraps of fabric for mama bear (or $1/2$ yard fabric)

Two 12" x 12" pieces of fabric for baby bear

Matching thread

Polyester fiberfill stuffing

Buttons for eyes: $3/4$" for large bear, $7/16$" for small bear or 18 mm safety eyes

Embroidery floss

1 yard $1/8$"-wide ribbon

INSTRUCTIONS

Note: All seam allowances are ¼".

Prewash and iron your fabrics. Prepare all patterns as instructed on page 10.

1. If using yardage, cut the fabric into $2^7/8$"-wide strips and then into $2^7/8$" squares. Cut these squares in half diagonally to form triangles.

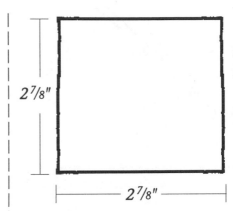

If using smaller scraps, use the triangle pattern to cut and mark the fabric into triangles.

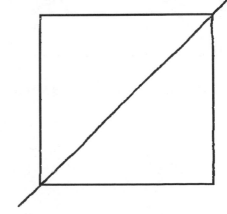

2. Right sides facing, stitch two triangles together along the long edges to form a square. Repeat until you have used up all of the triangles.

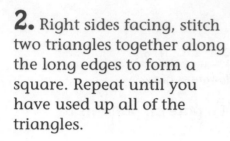

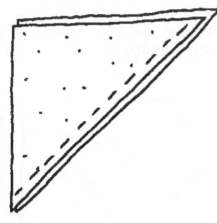

Press the seams to one side.

3. Stitch the squares into strips.

Press the seam allowances to one side.

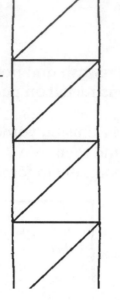

Sew the strips into rectangles, depending upon which pattern piece you are piecing to fit. Use the pattern pieces to decide how large to make the rectangles.

Press seam allowances to one side.

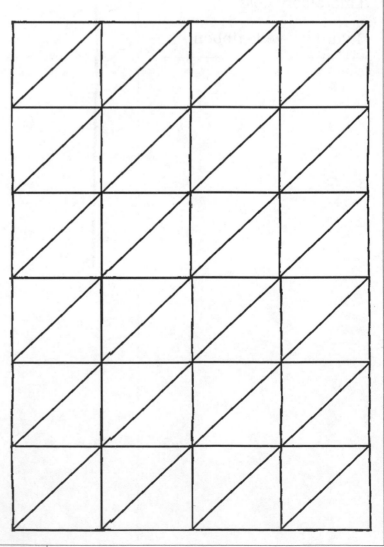

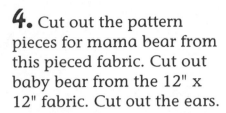

4. Cut out the pattern pieces for mama bear from this pieced fabric. Cut out baby bear from the 12" x 12" fabric. Cut out the ears.

5. Right sides together, stitch the two mama bear pieces together all the way around, leaving a 3" opening in the bear's side.

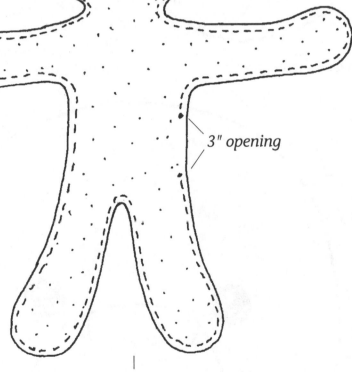

3" opening

Turn right side out. If using safety eyes, install them now.

Note: Use safety eyes for young children.

Repeat this procedure for baby bear.

6. Stuff a leg, then stitch across the top of the leg. Your zipper foot will make this easier.

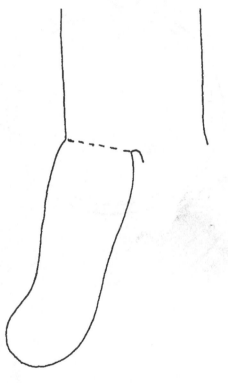

Repeat for the other leg.

Stuff the arms, head, and body. Ladder stitch the opening in the body closed.

7. Stuff baby bear. Stuff the arms, legs, and head first, then the body.

Ladder stitch the opening at the bear's side closed.

8. For both bears:

Gather stitch around the muzzle piece.

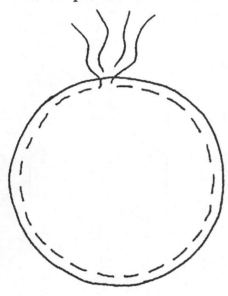

Pull up on the gather threads. Stuff with a ball of fiberfill. Stitch to the bears' faces.

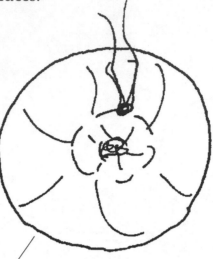

view is from back

9. Stitch the buttons to the bears' faces.

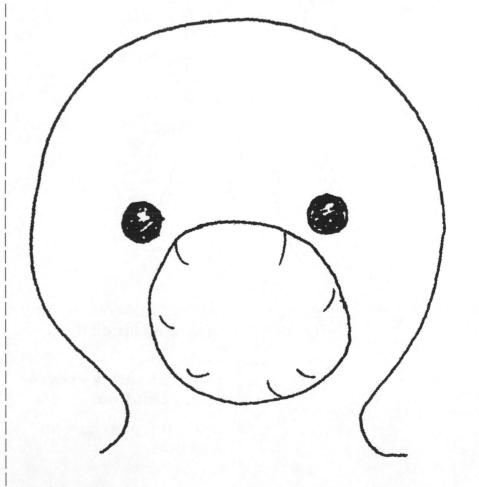

10. Place the nose pattern on the bears' faces. Trace. Embroider the bears' noses and mouths.

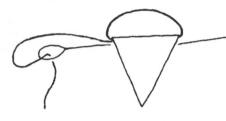

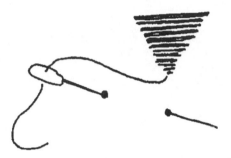

To end the embroidery thread, come out close to the muzzle and make a knot.

11. For each bear:

Stitch two ear pieces, right sides together.

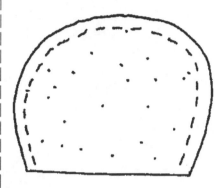

Turn right sides out. Turn the bottom raw edges ¼" to the inside. Whipstitch. Stitch to the bears' heads.

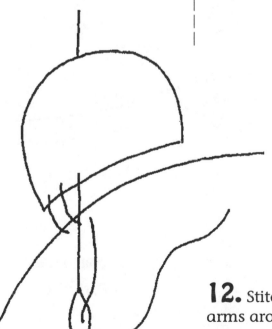

12. Stitch mama bear's arms around baby bear as shown in the photograph.

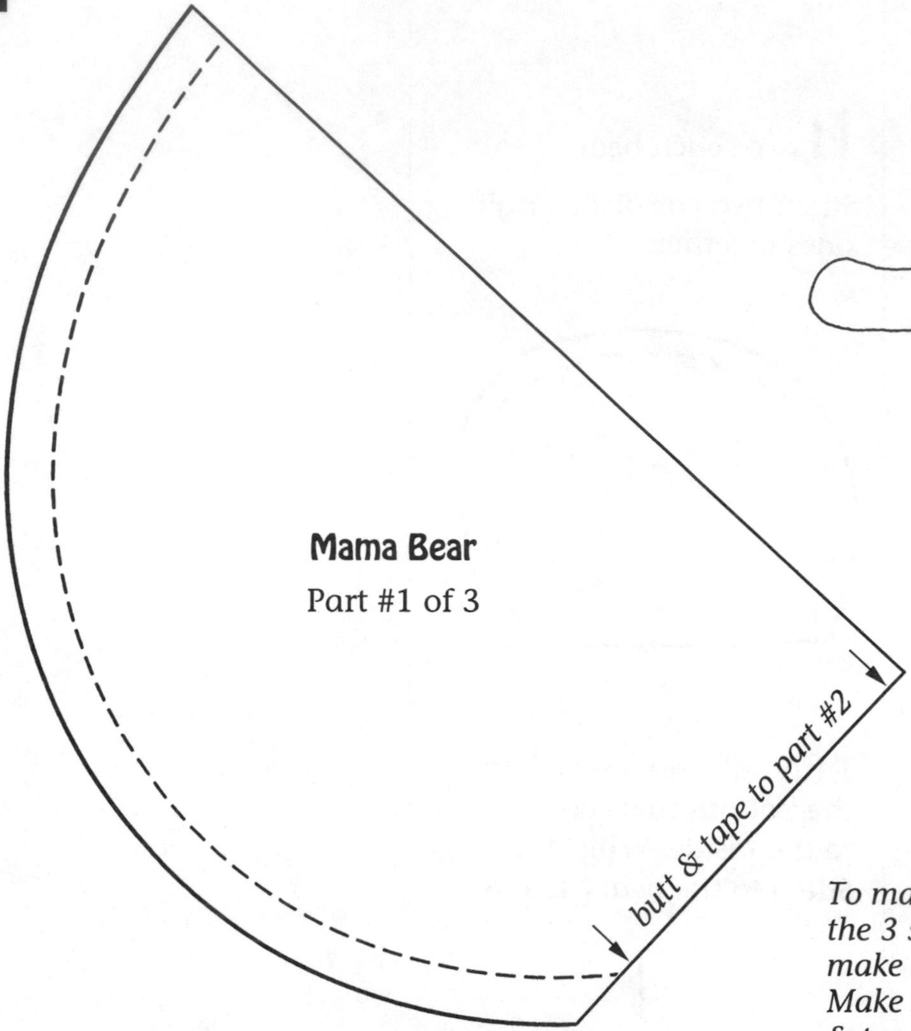

Mama Bear

Part #1 of 3

butt & tape to part #2

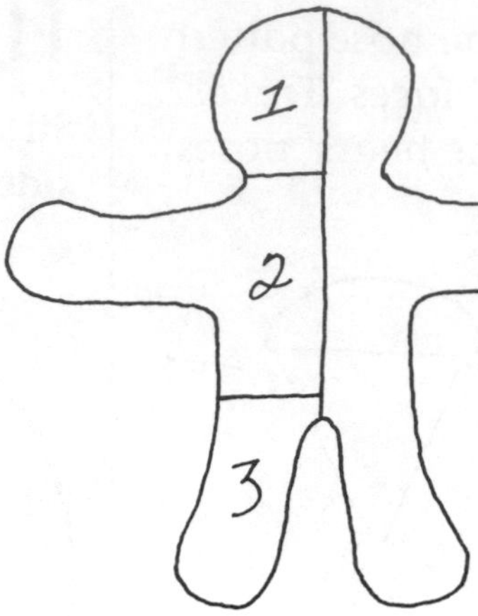

To make pattern: Butt & tape
the 3 sections together to
make half of the pattern.
Make a mirror image. Butt
& tape together.

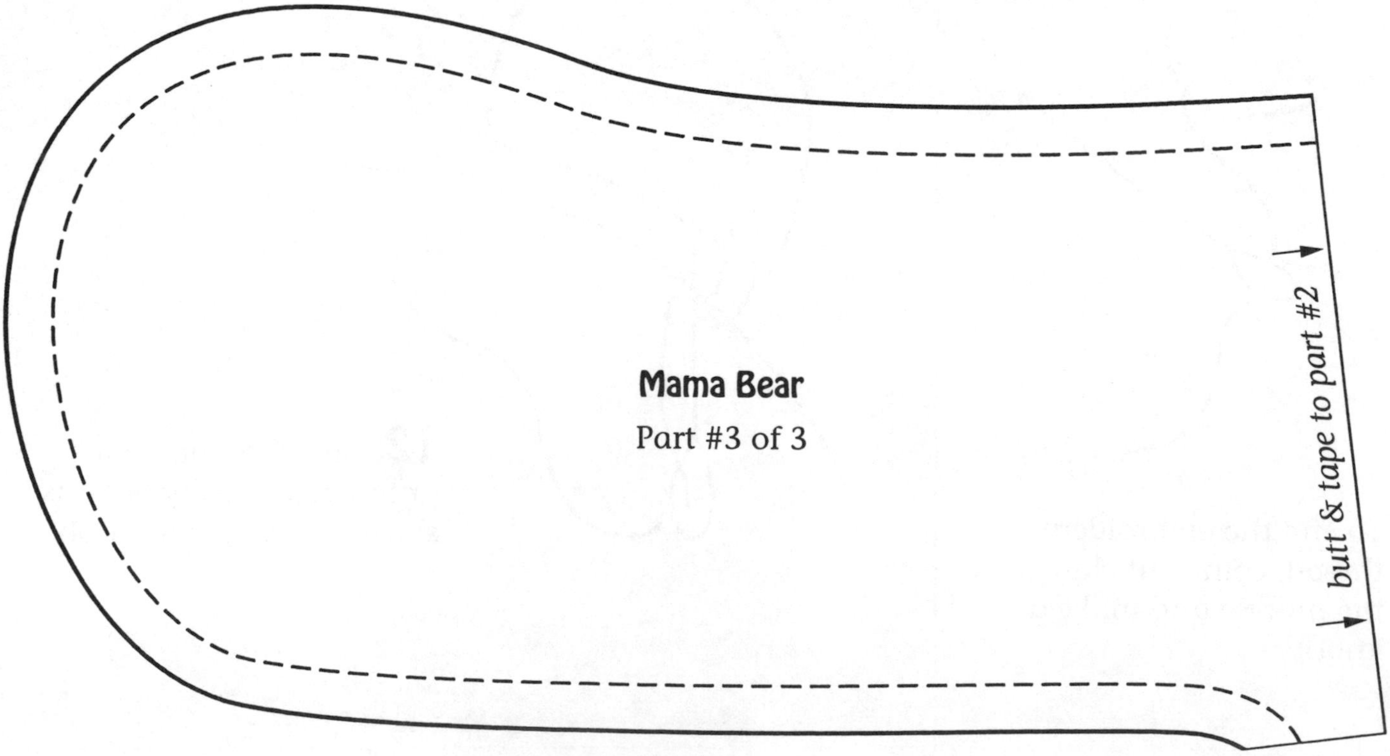

Mama Bear

Part #3 of 3

butt & tape to part #2

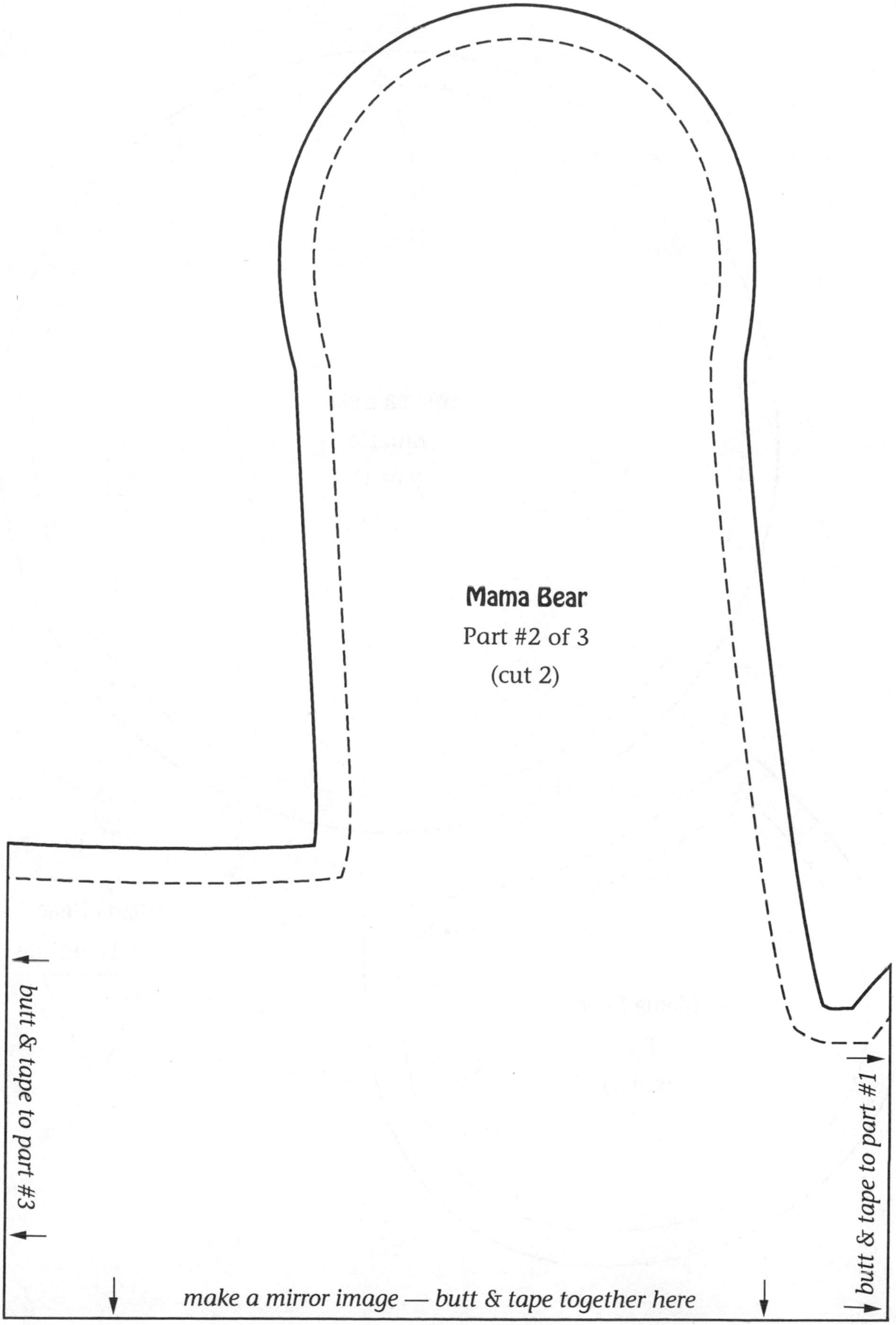

Mama Bear

Part #2 of 3

(cut 2)

butt & tape to part #3

butt & tape to part #1

make a mirror image — butt & tape together here

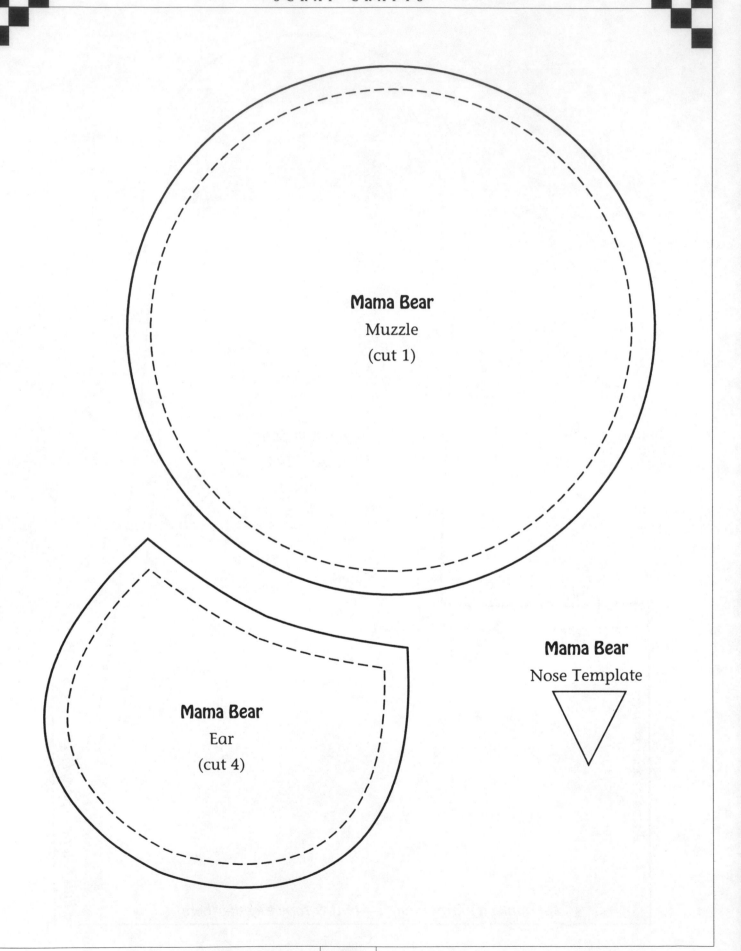

Mama Bear
Muzzle
(cut 1)

Mama Bear
Ear
(cut 4)

Mama Bear
Nose Template

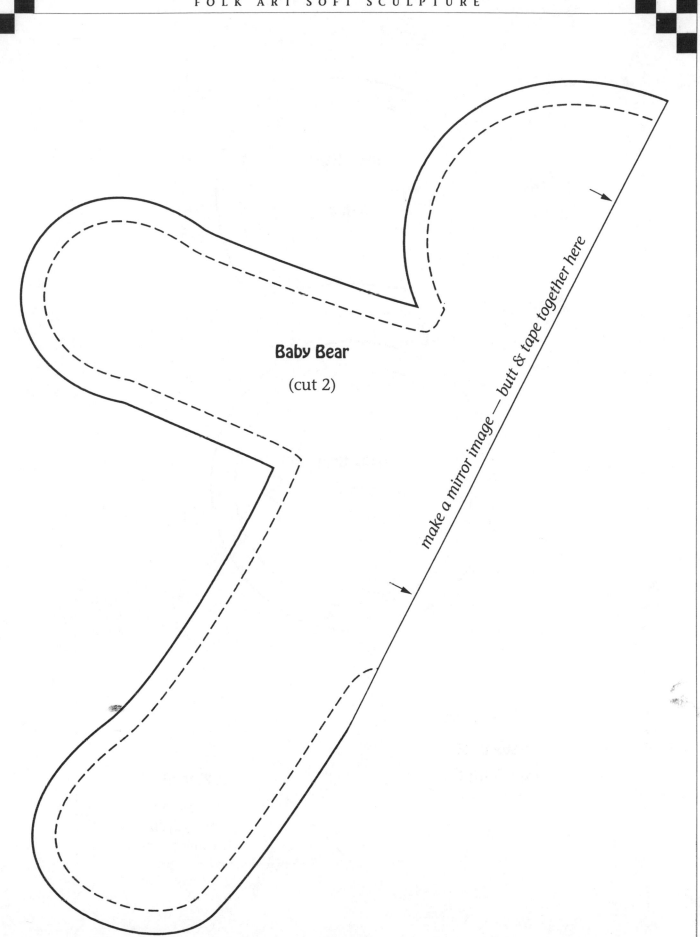

Baby Bear

(cut 2)

make a mirror image — butt & tape together here

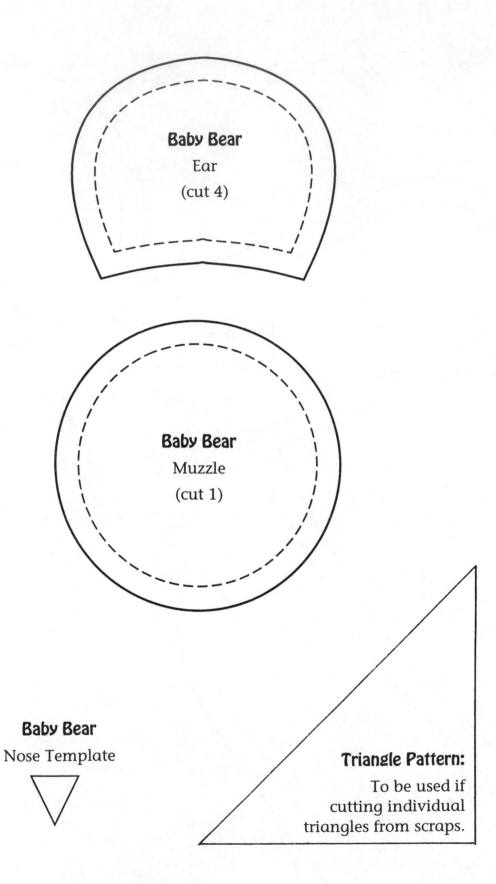

Baby Bear

Ear

(cut 4)

Baby Bear

Muzzle

(cut 1)

Baby Bear

Nose Template

Triangle Pattern:

To be used if
cutting individual
triangles from scraps.

Wearables & Accessories

QUILTED SUN/GARDEN HAT

Finished sizes: Small = 21", Medium = 22", Large = 23"

Linger in the sun or the garden while proudly wearing this attractive quilted hat. Use fabric with floral or country designs for a hat that's as fashionable as it is practical. Patterns for three sizes are given, as are instructions for measuring head sizes.

MATERIALS

Fabric scraps

³/₄ yard muslin

¹/₄ yard lining fabric

Matching thread

Batting scraps

Double-fold bias binding

One strip of fabric 4" wide and 44" or 45" long for flower

INSTRUCTIONS

Note: All seam allowances are ¼".

Prewash and iron your fabrics. Prepare patterns as instructed on page 10.

To determine the hat size, measure the head size as shown.

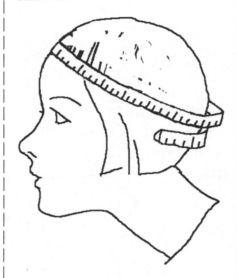

1. Cut one hat body and one hat top from lining fabric.

2. Right sides facing, stitch the short edges of the hat lining together.

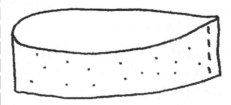

3. Right sides facing, pin the lining top to the body lining. Stitch.

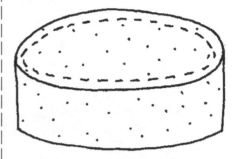

4. Lay the hat top and hat body patterns on the muslin. Cut the muslin at least 1" larger than the patterns. Repeat for the brim pattern piece, repeating until you have twelve brim pieces.

Lay all of the muslin pieces, except those for the brim, on the batting and cut the batting into pieces roughly the same size as the muslin pieces.

5. Crazy patch the hat top, body, and the twelve brim pieces by following the instructions on page 10. Don't use batting for the brim pieces, use only muslin.

6. Right (crazy-patched) sides facing, stitch the two short ends of the hat body together.

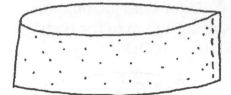

Right sides together, pin the crazy-patched hat top to the crazy-patched hat body, easing to fit. Stitch.

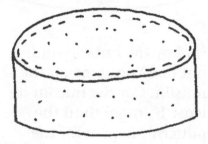

7. Right sides facing, stitch six crazy-patched hat brim pieces together to form an incomplete circle. Repeat with the remaining six hat brim pieces.

and so on

Right sides facing, pin and stitch the two brim rings together along the large, outside circle.

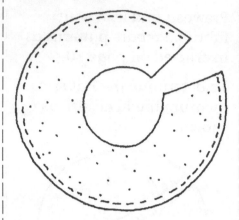

Right sides facing, match and pin the two raw edges of the brim to complete the circle.

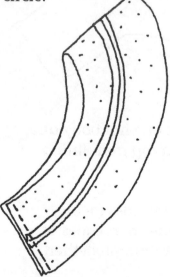

Turn right side out.

Press the brim. Baste the raw edges of the smaller, inside circle together.

8. Turn the crazy-patched hat body/top right side out. Put the hat body/top lining inside so that the wrong sides are together. Baste the raw edges together.

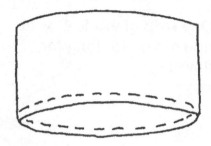

9. Pin the hat brim to the hat body/top, with the brim against the crazy-patched side of the hat body. Stitch.

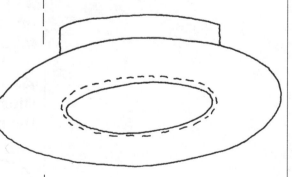

10. Unfold the bias tape. Stitch one edge to the hat body/brim seam you just stitched. Turn up the raw end about ¼" at the beginning of the stitching and continue around the seam. When you come around to the beginning again, overlap the bias binding ½" or so.

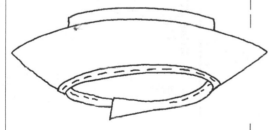

Fold the bias binding over the raw edges. Topstitch.

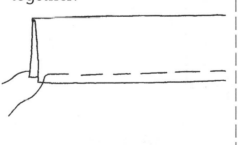

11. Wrong sides facing, baste the long raw edges of the flower fabric strip together.

Pull up on the gather stitches to shorten the strip by about one half.

To begin at the center of the flower, fold one edge down.

Roll the strip around this center.

Hand stitch through the layers to secure them. Do not cut the thread.

Roll the strip around the center a few more times. Stitch. Repeat until you have used the entire strip. Fold the raw edge at the end to the inside of the flower.

Fold up the hat brim at the front. Stitch the flower through the brim and the hat body.

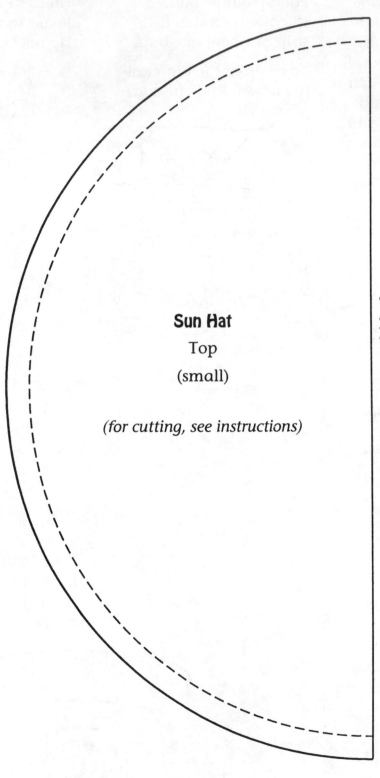

Sun Hat

Top

(small)

(for cutting, see instructions)

to make pattern, cut on fold of paper

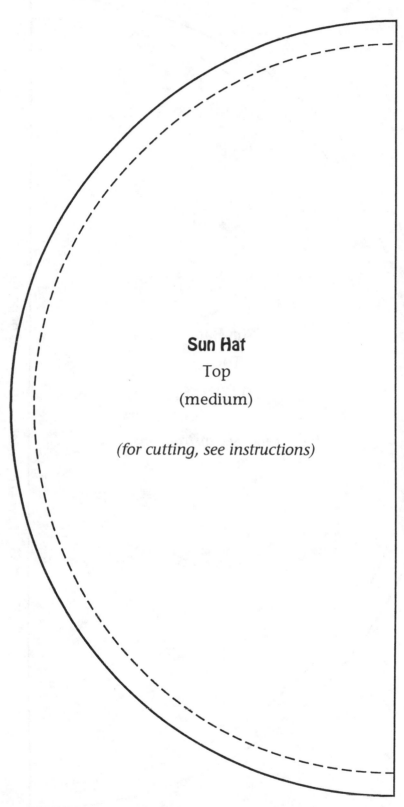

Sun Hat

Top

(medium)

(for cutting, see instructions)

to make pattern, cut on fold of paper

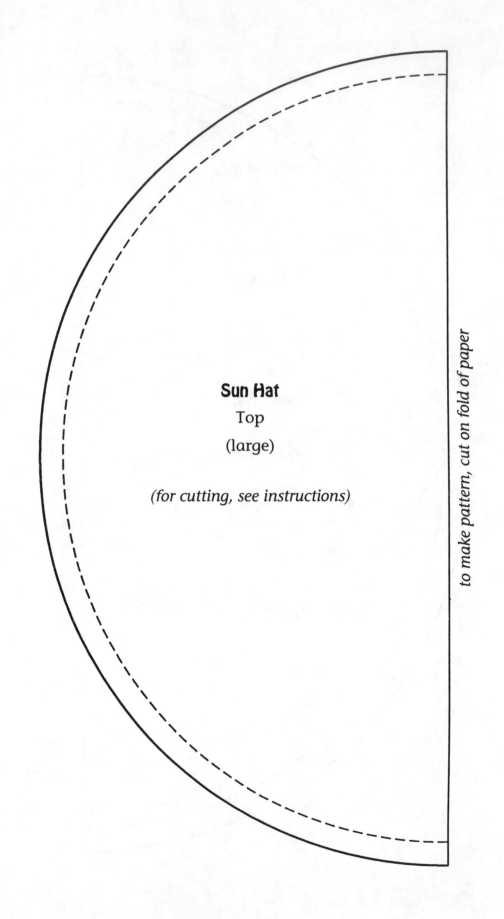

Sun Hat

Top

(large)

(for cutting, see instructions)

to make pattern, cut on fold of paper

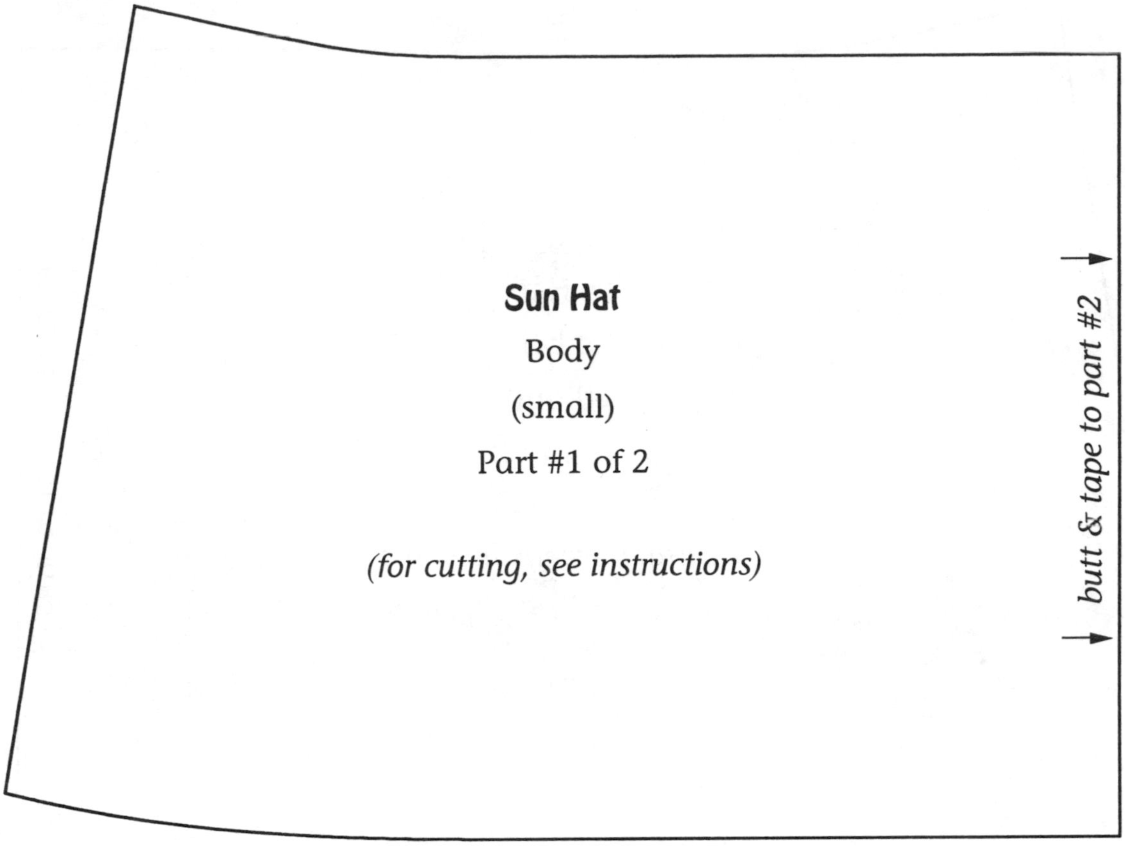

Sun Hat

Body

(small)

Part #1 of 2

(for cutting, see instructions)

butt & tape to part #2

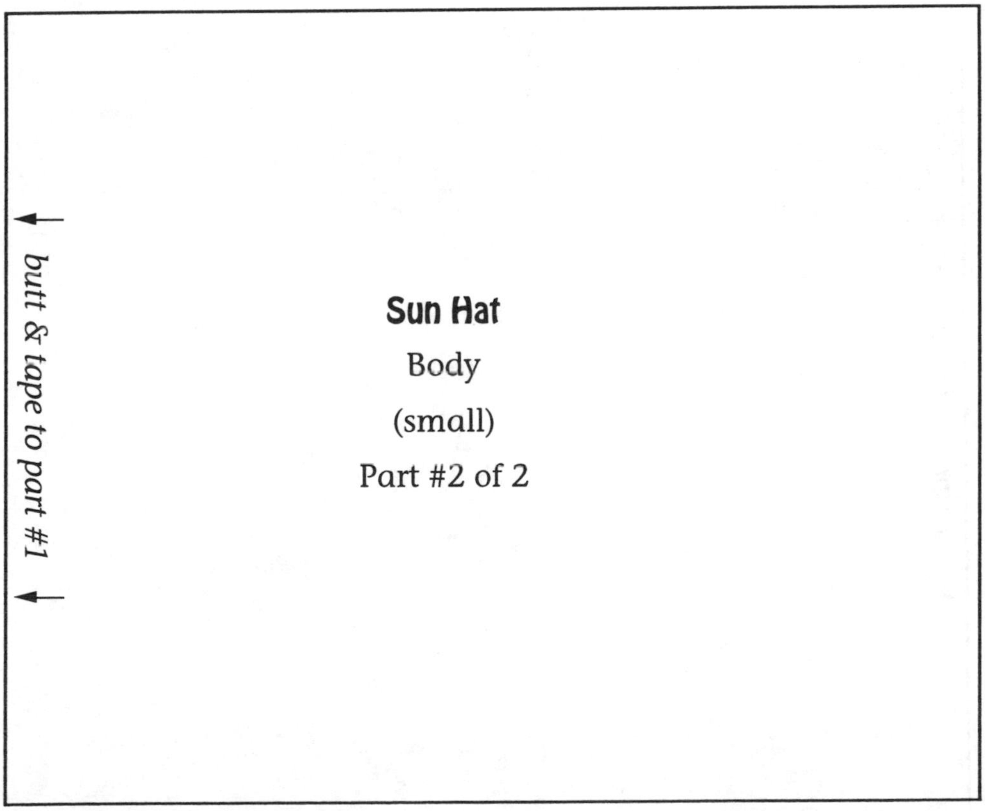

Sun Hat

Body

(small)

Part #2 of 2

butt & tape to part #1

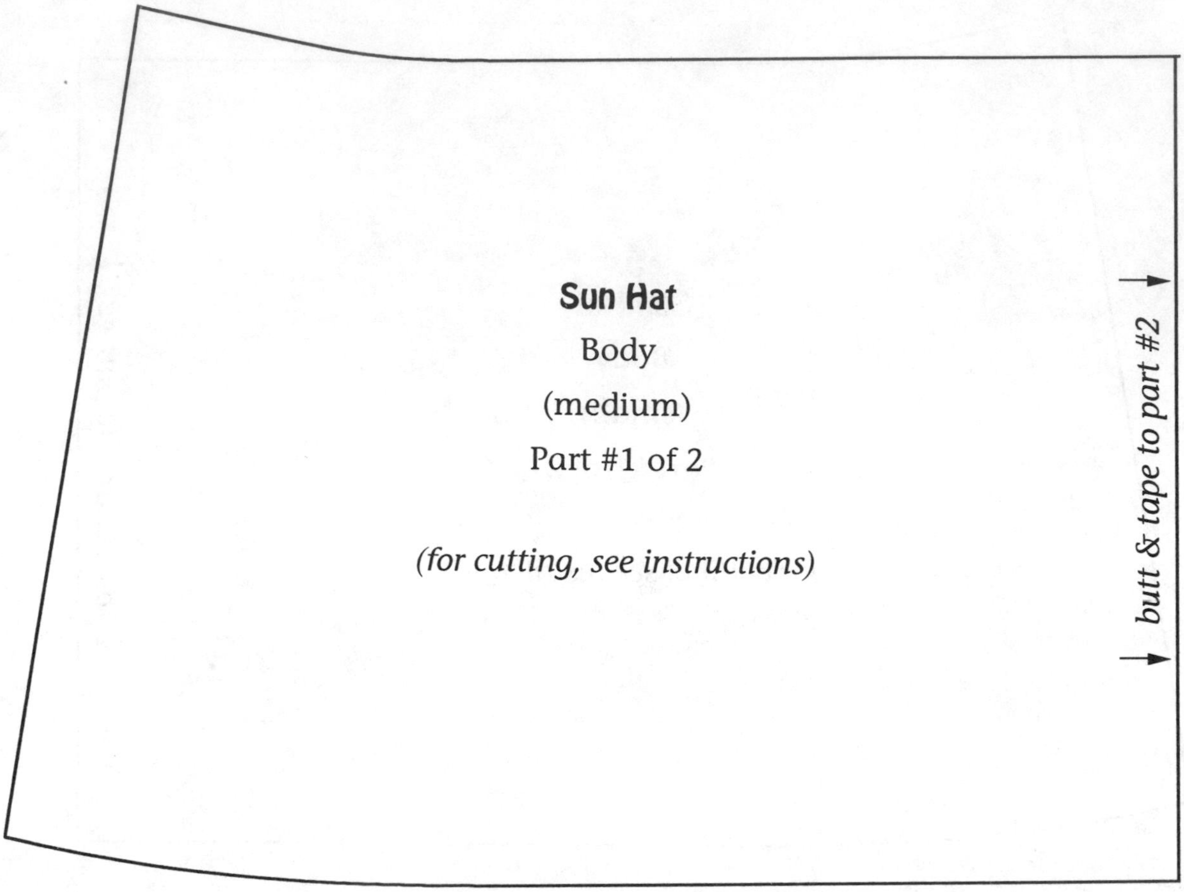

Sun Hat

Body

(medium)

Part #1 of 2

(for cutting, see instructions)

butt & tape to part #2

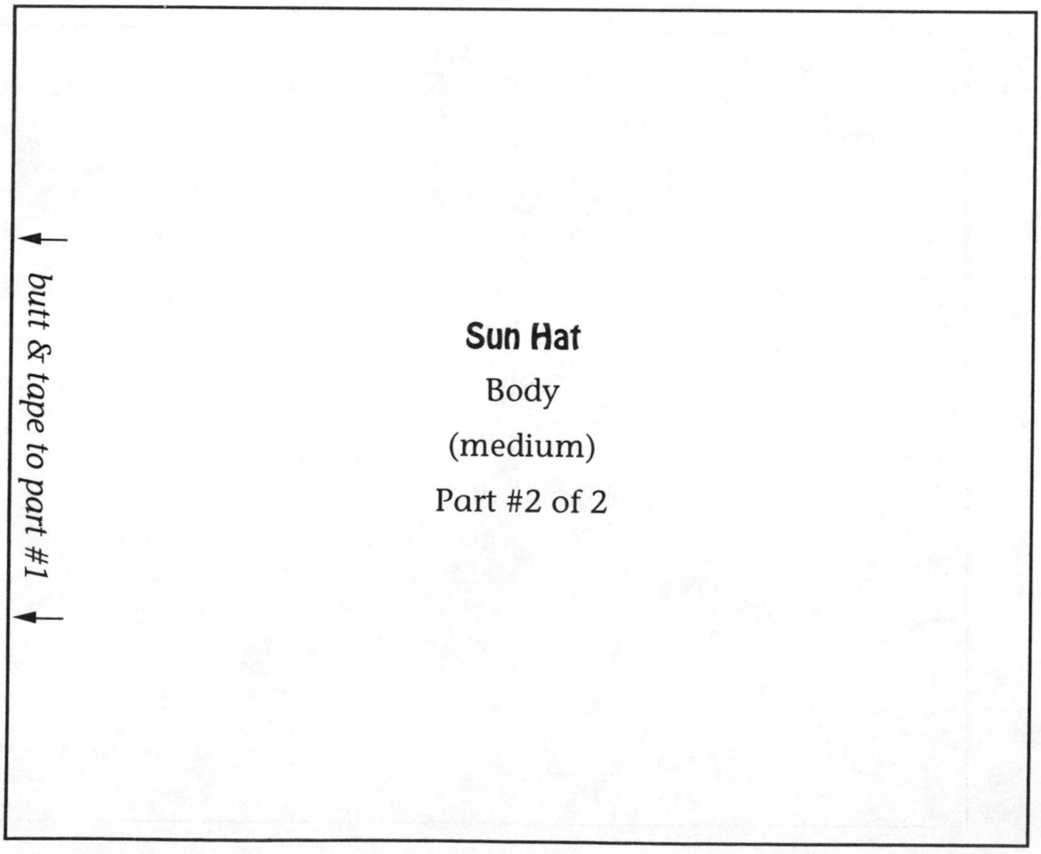

Sun Hat

Body

(medium)

Part #2 of 2

butt & tape to part #1

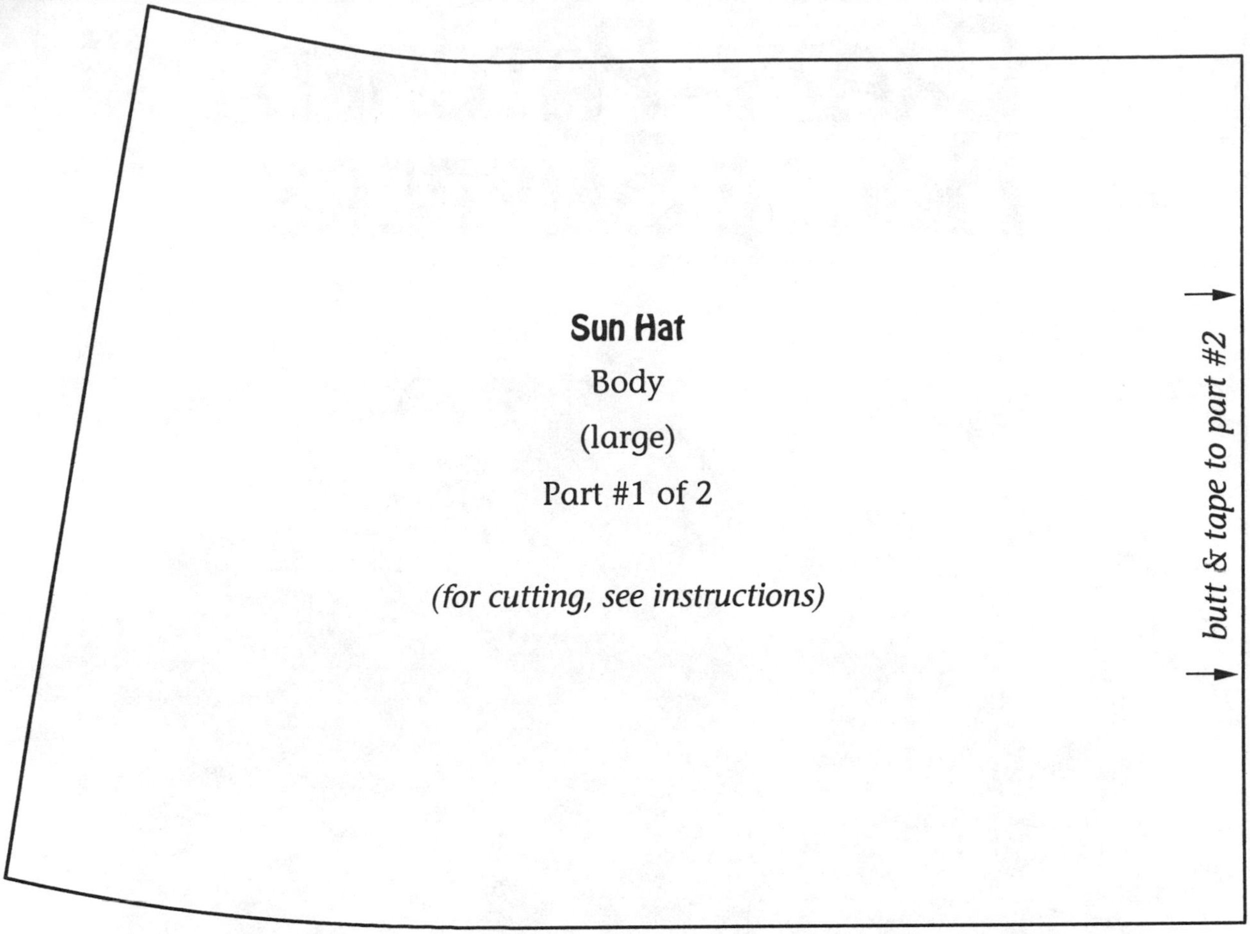

Sun Hat

Body

(large)

Part #1 of 2

(for cutting, see instructions)

butt & tape to part #2

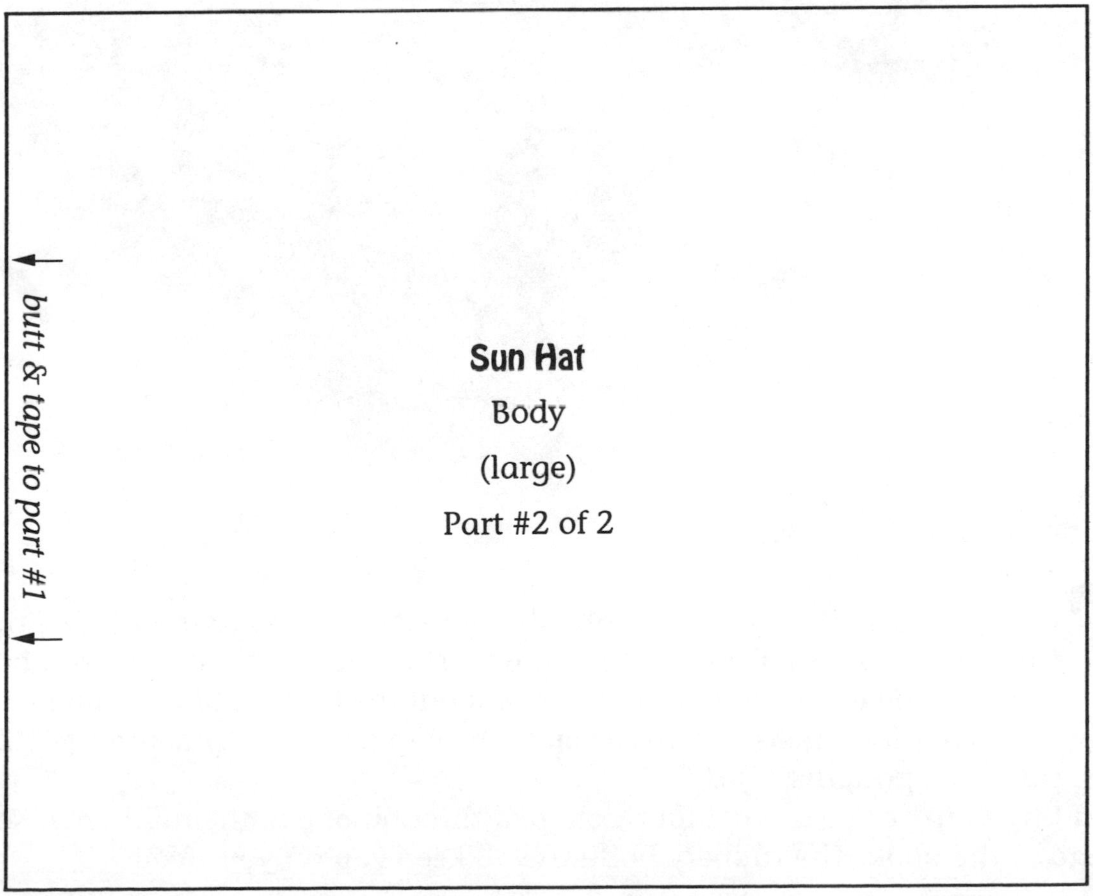

butt & tape to part #1

Sun Hat

Body

(large)

Part #2 of 2

CRAZY-PATCHED HOUSE SLIPPERS

These cozy and comfy slippers are also non-skid thanks to their Jiffy Grip™ soles. Stitch up slippers for your entire family using this easy fitting method: Simply measure the length of your foot and cut out the pattern of the same length. For example, if your foot measures 10" from the heel to tip of the toes, use the 10" sole and slipper side patterns.

Find Jiffy Grip™ at your local fabric shop or through one of the mail order sources at the end of the book. The rubbery bottoms will keep you on your feet!

 MATERIALS

Fabric scraps

³/₈ yard muslin

³/₈ yard lining fabric

Matching thread

Jiffy Grip™

Batting scraps

⁵/₈ yard ribbon

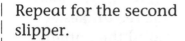 INSTRUCTIONS

Note: All seam allowances are ¹/₄" unless otherwise specified.

Prewash and iron your fabrics. Prepare patterns as instructed on page 10.

1. Lay the sole pattern on top of the muslin. Cut a rectangle from the muslin larger than the sole pattern. Repeat for one slipper side. Flip the slipper side pattern and repeat.

Repeat for the second slipper.

Use the muslin rectangles as patterns to cut three pieces of batting, one for the sole and one for each side piece. Repeat for the second slipper.

2. Following the instructions on page 10, crazy patch the two slipper side pieces for each slipper.

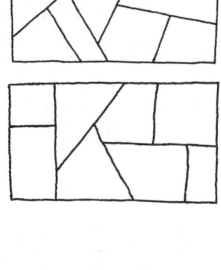

3. Lay the slipper side pattern on top of the pieced slipper side rectangles. Trace around the pattern. Transfer the dot at the front of the shoe side to the muslin. Baste a scant 1/4" from the raw edges. Cut along the traced lines.

Repeat for the second slipper side, remembering to flip the pattern.

4. Right sides facing, stitch the shoe sides together along the back seam and the front seam. For the front, start at the dot and stitch down as shown.

Repeat for the second slipper.

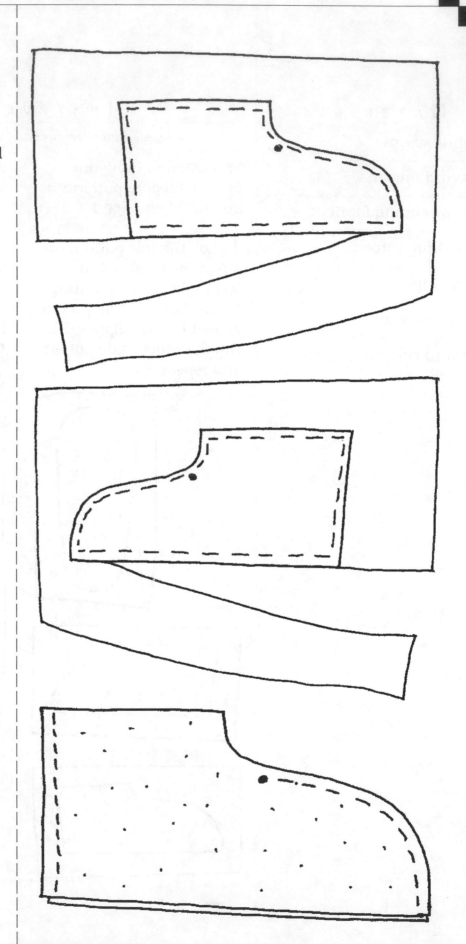

5. Cut two slipper sole bottoms from the Jiffy Grip™. Baste the piece of batting to the wrong side of each of the Jiffy Grip™ pieces.

With the Jiffy Grip™ facing the right side of the slipper sides, pin and stitch the sole to the pieced slipper sides. Repeat for the second slipper.

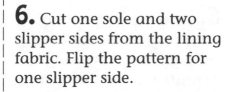

6. Cut one sole and two slipper sides from the lining fabric. Flip the pattern for one slipper side.

Right sides facing, stitch the shoe side lining pieces together along the back seam and front seams. For the front, start at the dot and stitch down as shown.

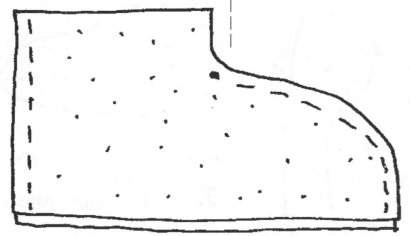

Repeat for the second slipper.

Right sides facing, pin the slipper sole lining to the slipper sides lining. Stitch, leaving a 3"-long opening along one side for turning.

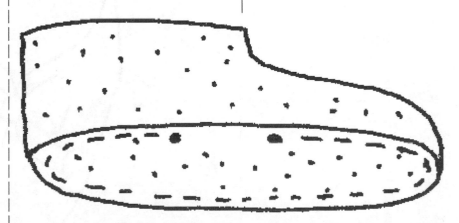

Repeat for the second slipper.

7. With one slipper wrong side out and one slipper lining right side out, put the lining inside the slipper. Match and pin the top raw edges. Stitch from the dot, around the top edge of the slipper, and back to the dot.

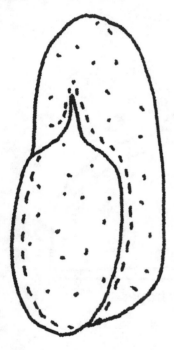

Repeat for the second slipper.

8. Turn the slipper and lining right side out through the 3" opening. Topstitch along the opening in the slipper lining.

Repeat for the second slipper.

9. Push the lining into the slipper.

10. Cut the ribbon in half. Make two bows. Stitch one to each slipper.

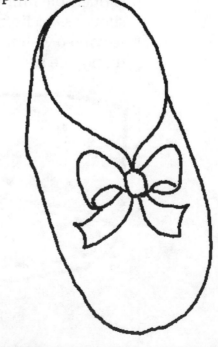

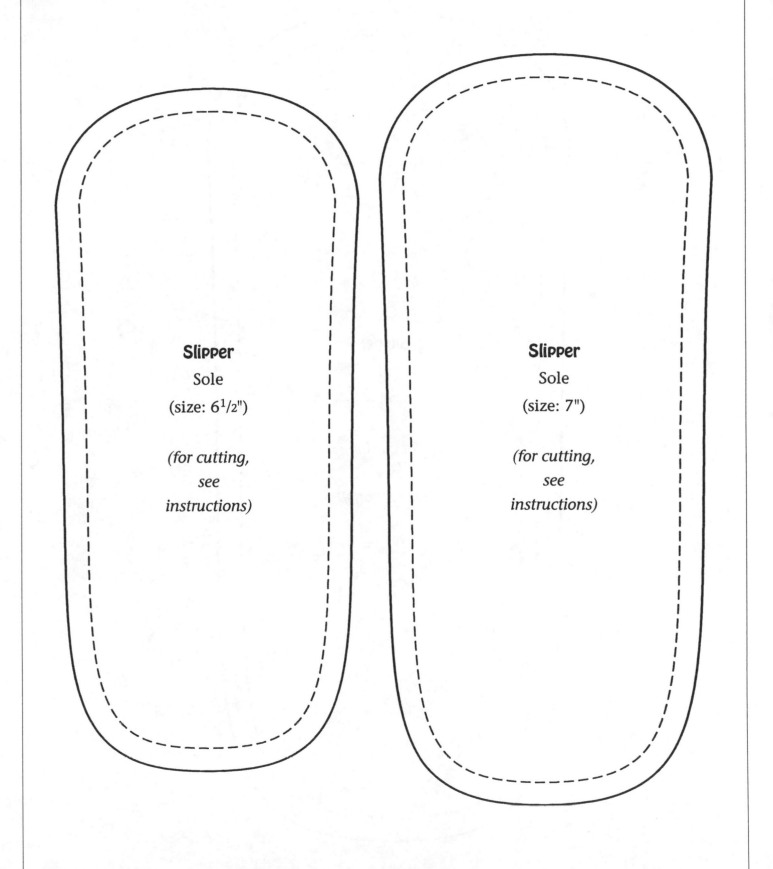

Slipper
Sole
(size: 6$\frac{1}{2}$")

*(for cutting,
see
instructions)*

Slipper
Sole
(size: 7")

*(for cutting,
see
instructions)*

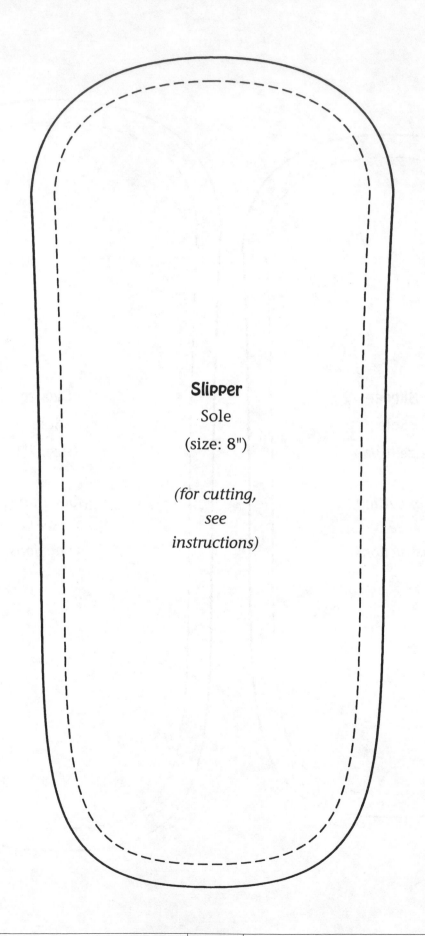

Slipper

Sole

(size: 8")

*(for cutting,
see
instructions)*

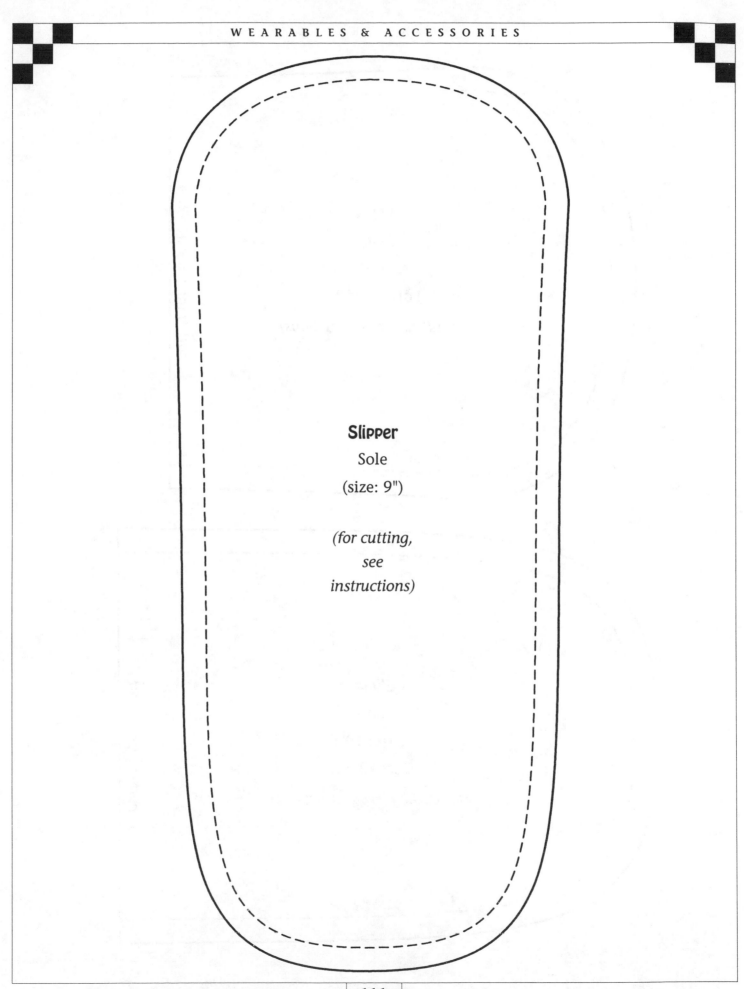

Slipper

Sole

(size: 9")

(for cutting,
see
instructions)

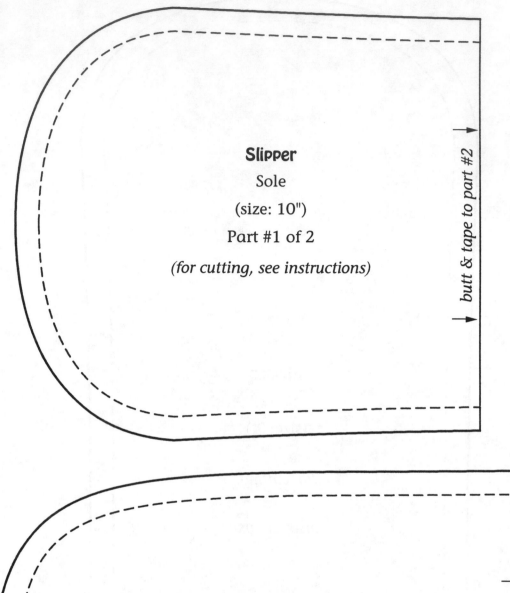

Slipper

Sole

(size: 10")

Part #1 of 2

(for cutting, see instructions)

butt & tape to part #2

Slipper

Sole

(size: 10")

Part #2 of 2

(for cutting, see instructions)

butt & tape to part #1

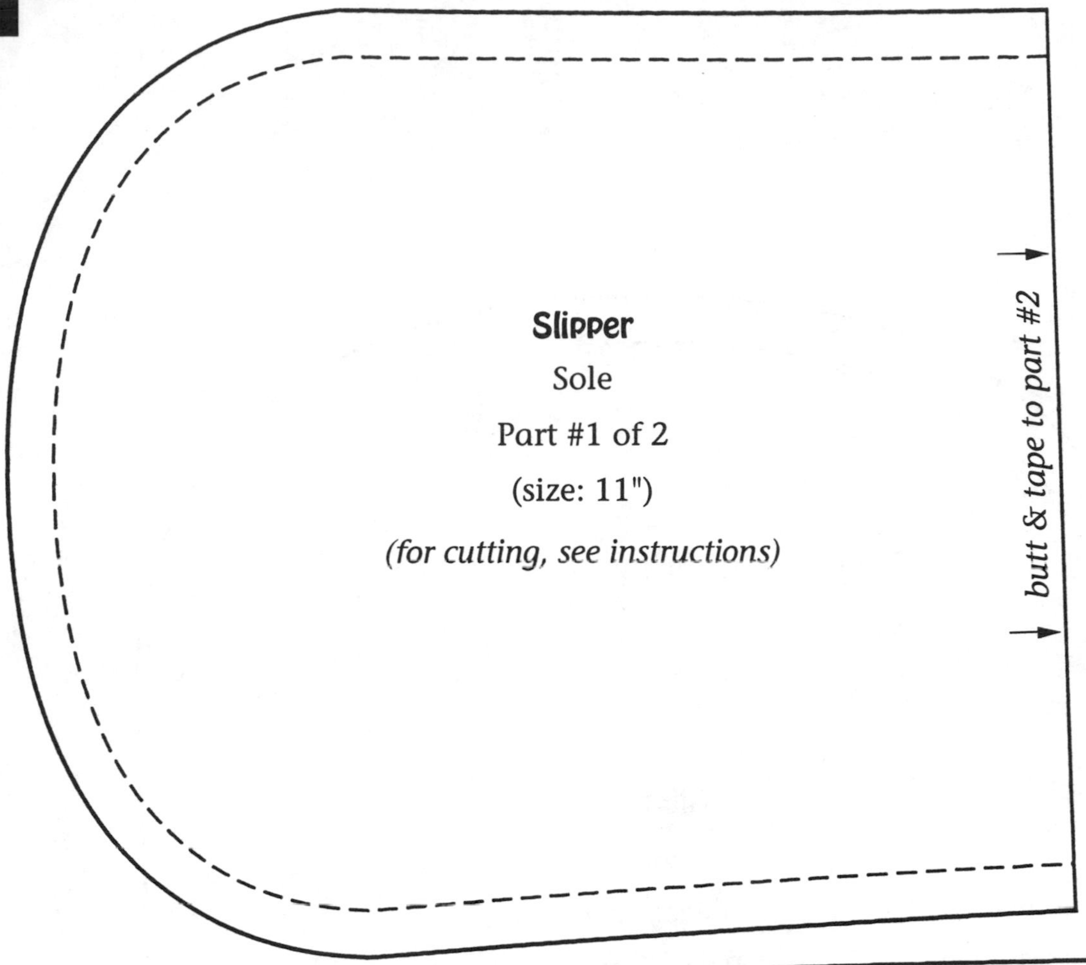

Slipper

Sole

Part #1 of 2

(size: 11")

(for cutting, see instructions)

butt & tape to part #2

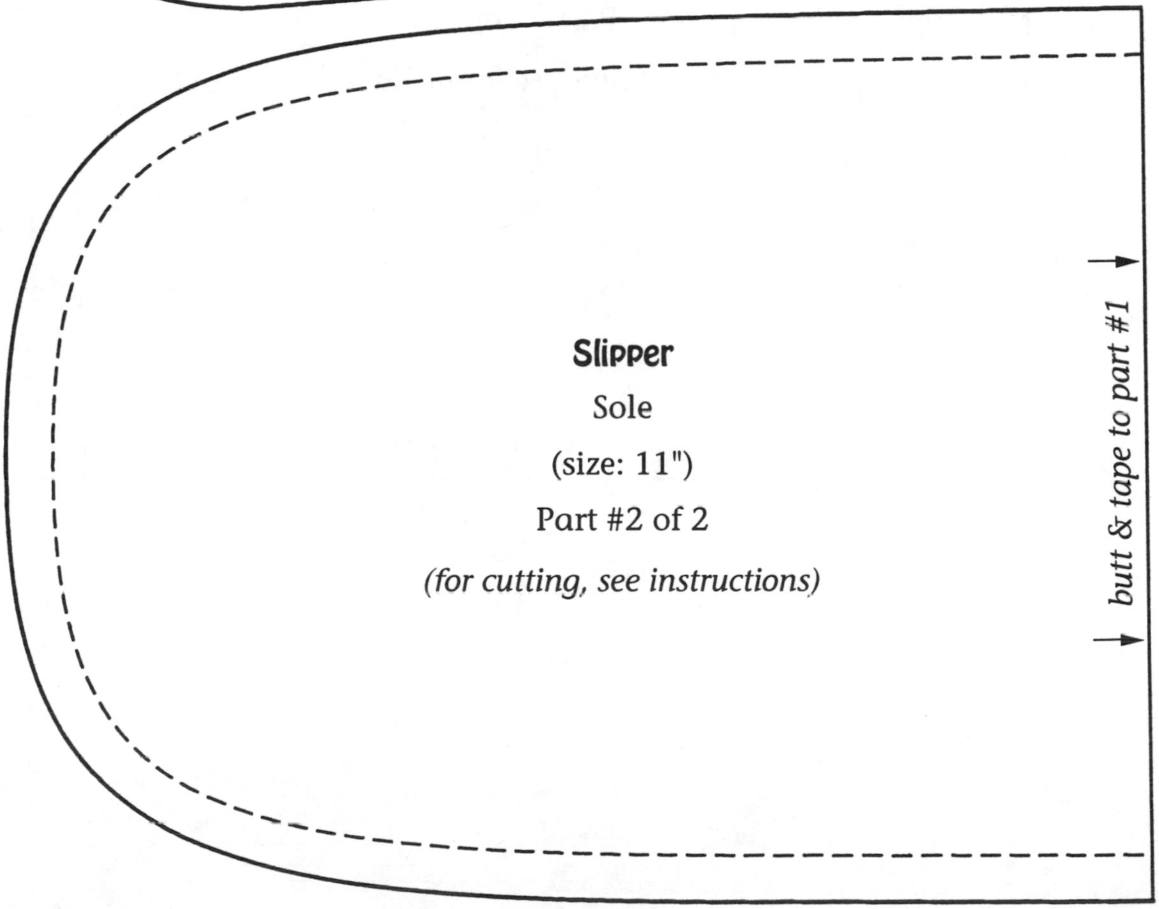

Slipper

Sole

(size: 11")

Part #2 of 2

(for cutting, see instructions)

butt & tape to part #1

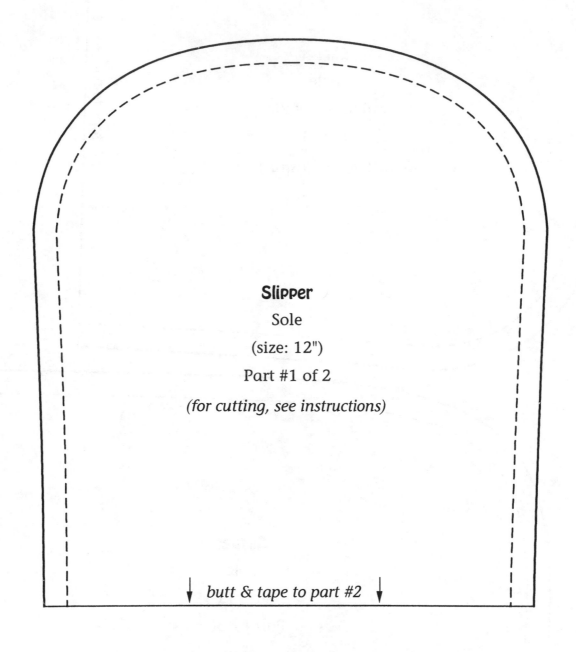

Slipper

Sole

(size: 12")

Part #1 of 2

(for cutting, see instructions)

↓ *butt & tape to part #2* ↓

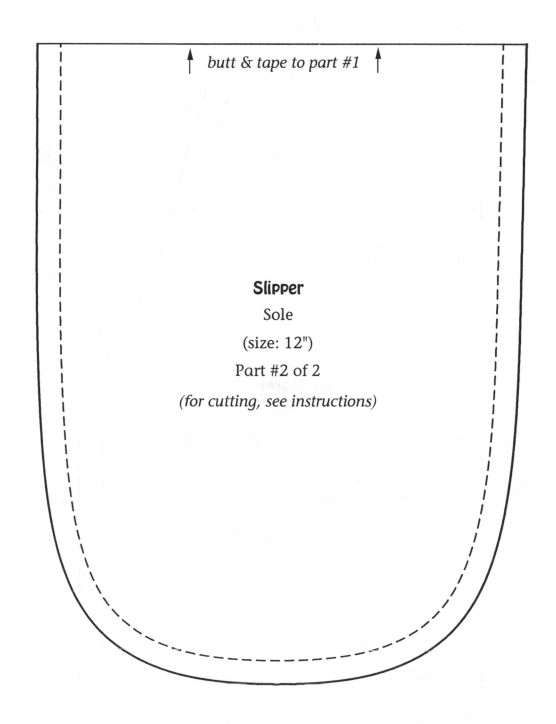

butt & tape to part #1

Slipper

Sole

(size: 12")

Part #2 of 2

(for cutting, see instructions)

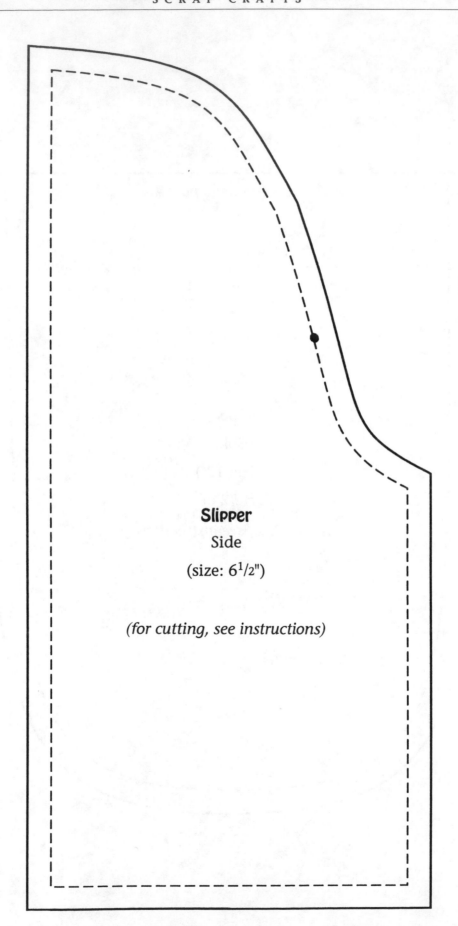

Slipper

Side

(size: 6^1/$_2$")

(for cutting, see instructions)

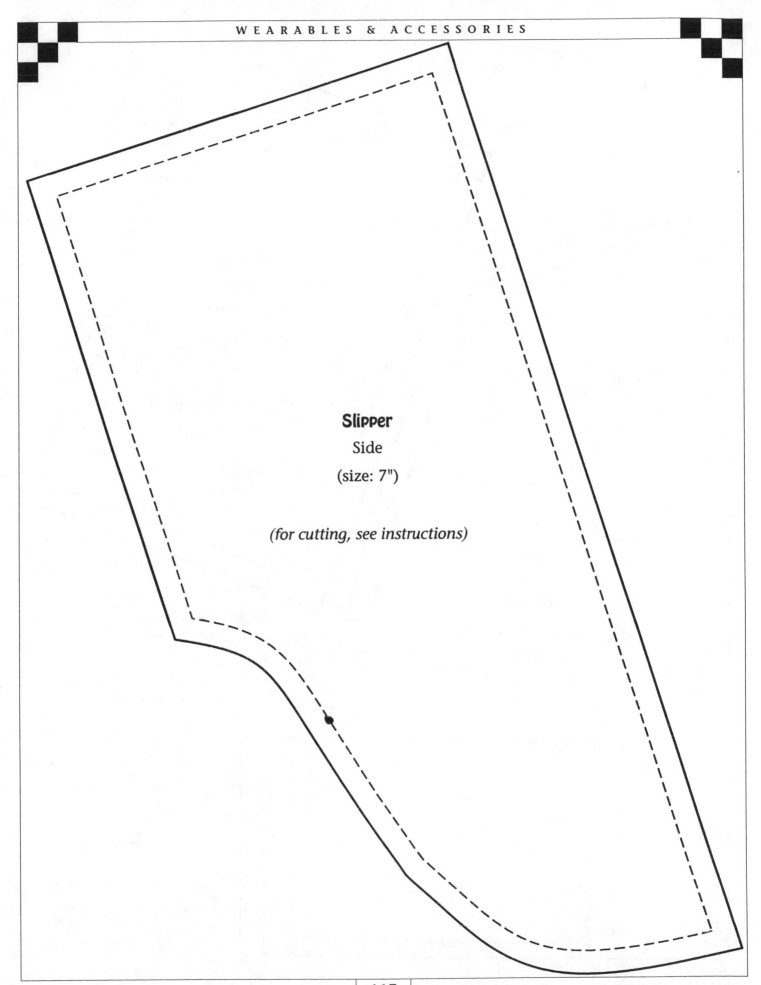

Slipper

Side

(size: 7")

(for cutting, see instructions)

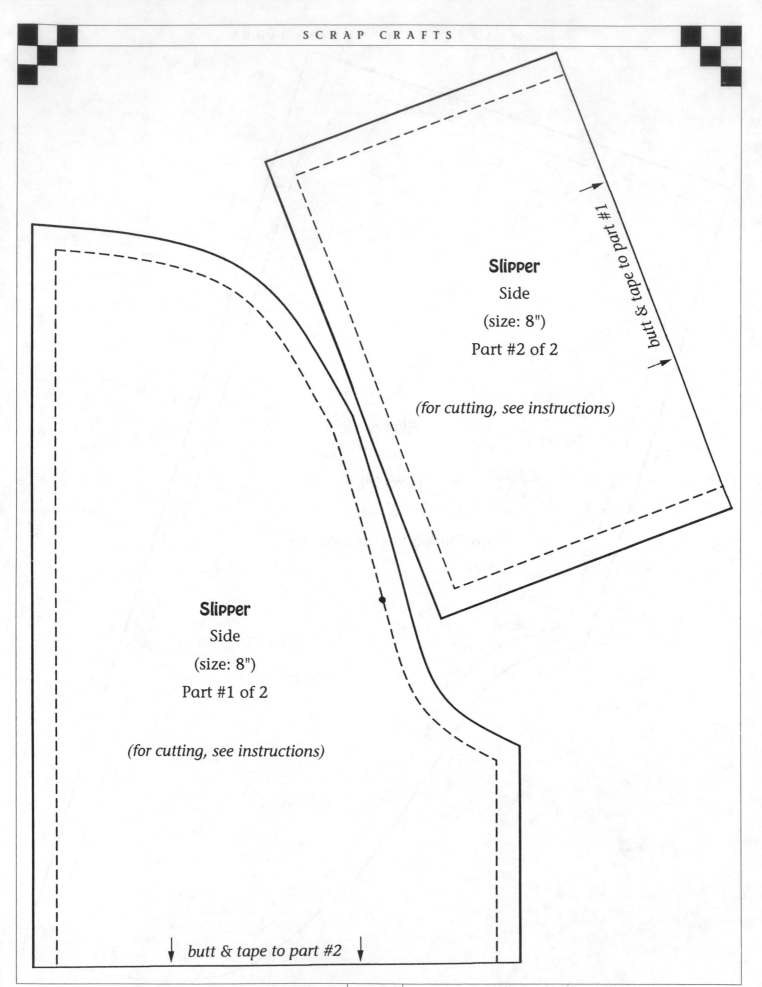

Slipper
Side
(size: 8")
Part #2 of 2

(for cutting, see instructions)

butt & tape to part #1

Slipper
Side
(size: 8")
Part #1 of 2

(for cutting, see instructions)

↓ *butt & tape to part #2* ↓

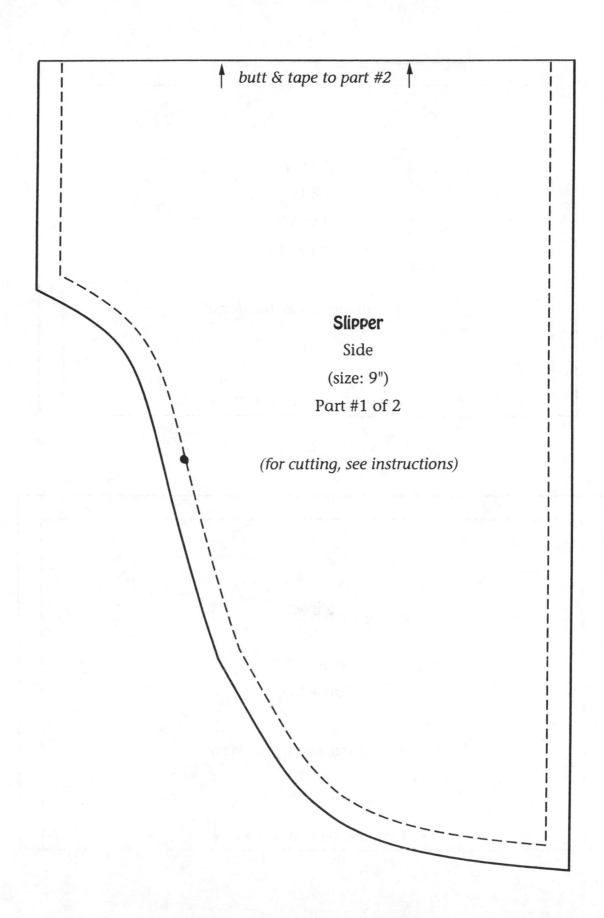

butt & tape to part #2

Slipper

Side

(size: 9")

Part #1 of 2

(for cutting, see instructions)

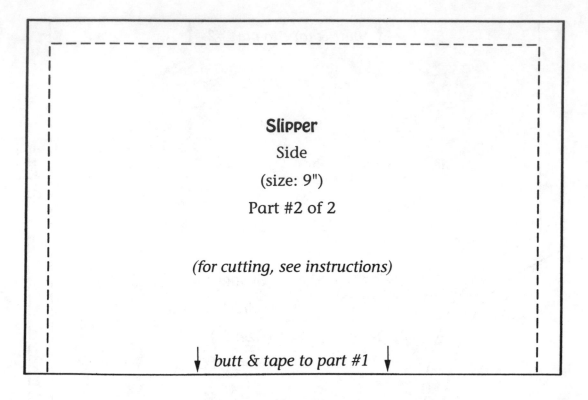

Slipper

Side

(size: 9")

Part #2 of 2

(for cutting, see instructions)

↓ *butt & tape to part #1* ↓

Slipper

Side

(size: 10")

Part #2 of 2

(for cutting, see instructions)

↓ *butt & tape to part #1* ↓

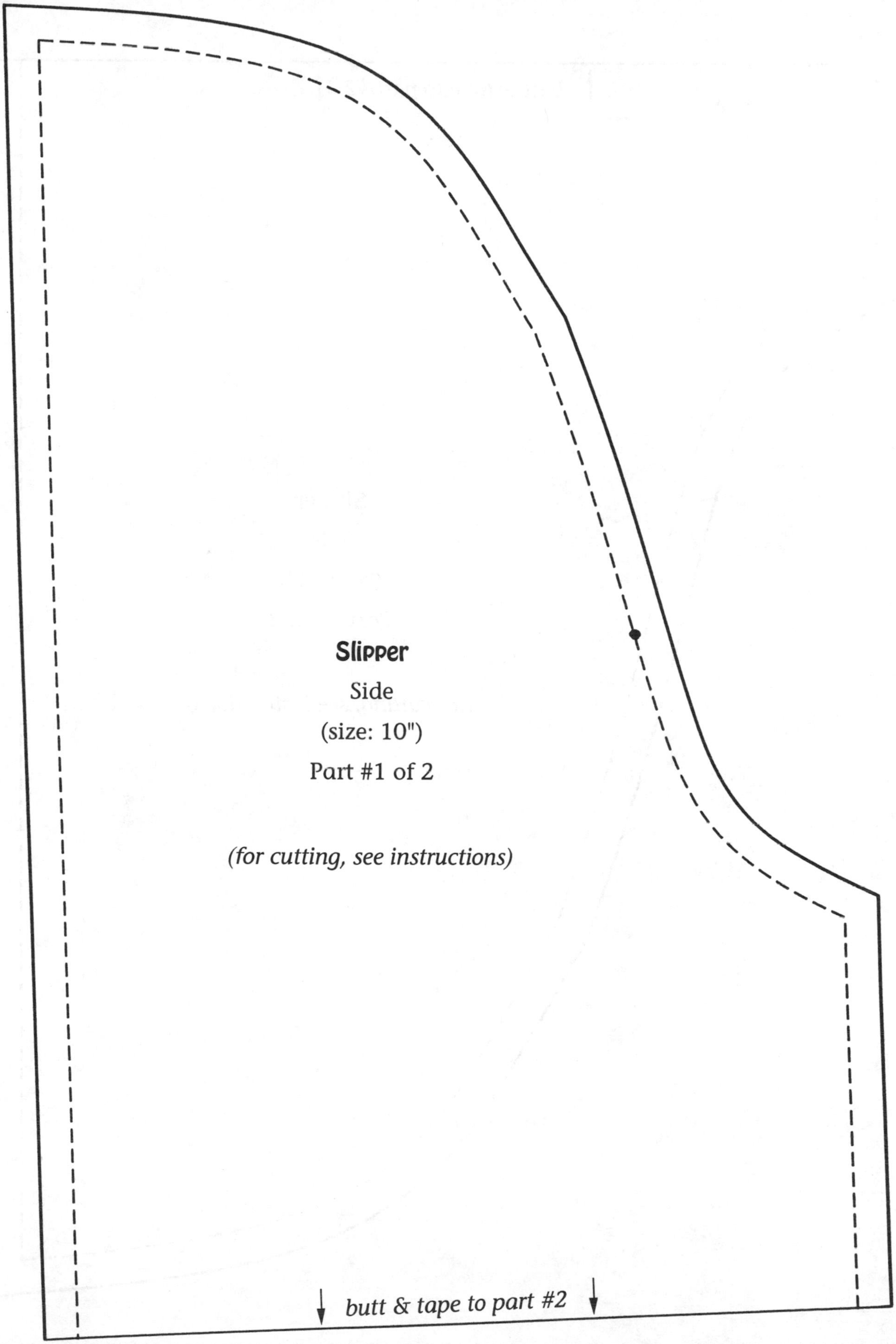

Slipper

Side

(size: 10")

Part #1 of 2

(for cutting, see instructions)

↓ *butt & tape to part #2* ↓

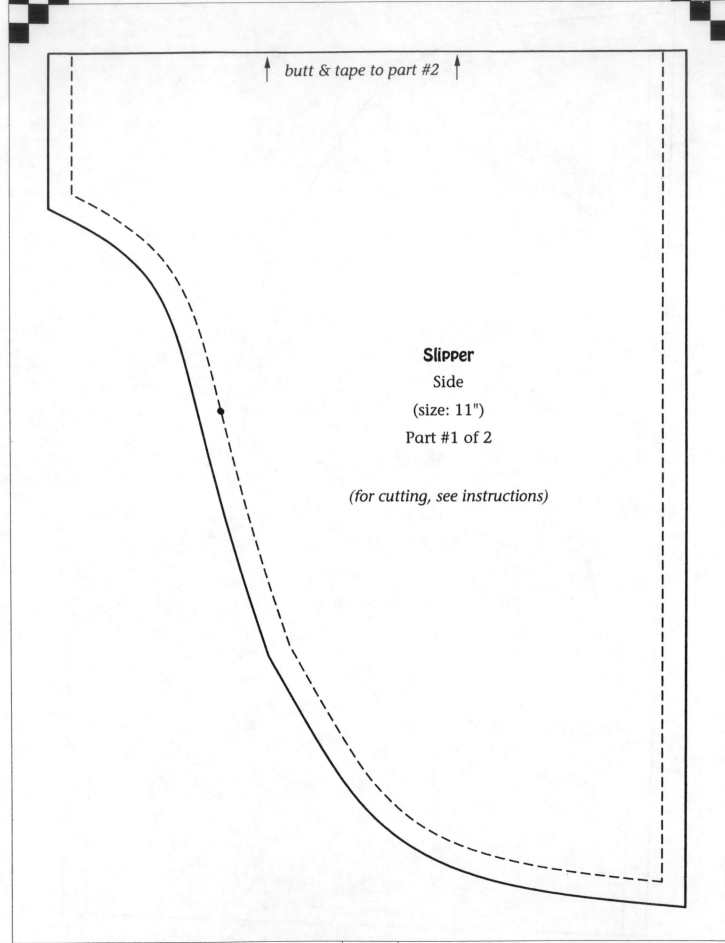

butt & tape to part #2

Slipper
Side
(size: 11")
Part #1 of 2

(for cutting, see instructions)

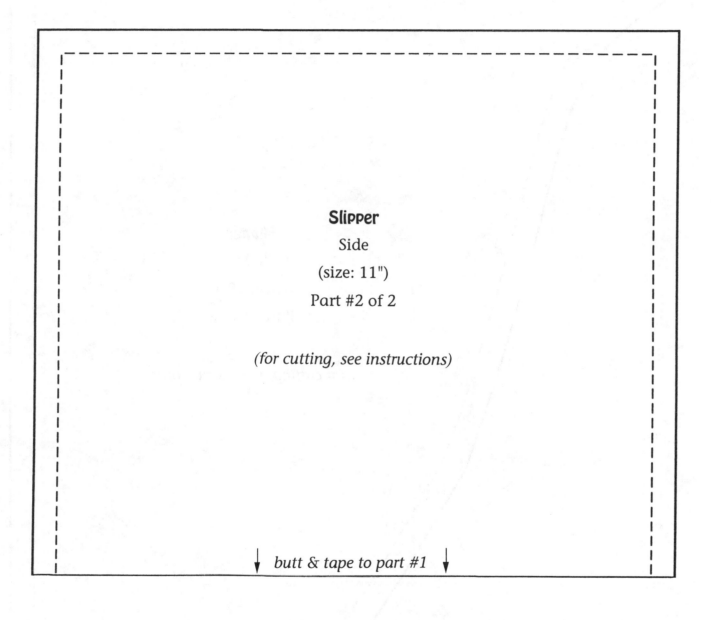

Slipper

Side

(size: 11")

Part #2 of 2

(for cutting, see instructions)

↓ *butt & tape to part #1* ↓

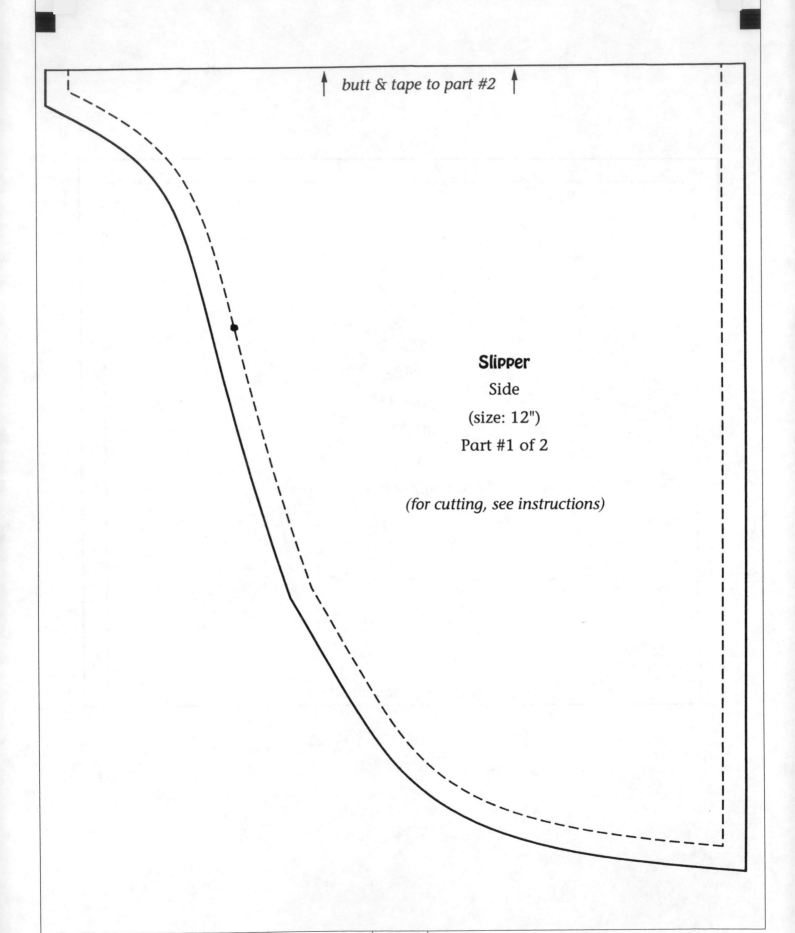

butt & tape to part #2

Slipper
Side
(size: 12")
Part #1 of 2

(for cutting, see instructions)

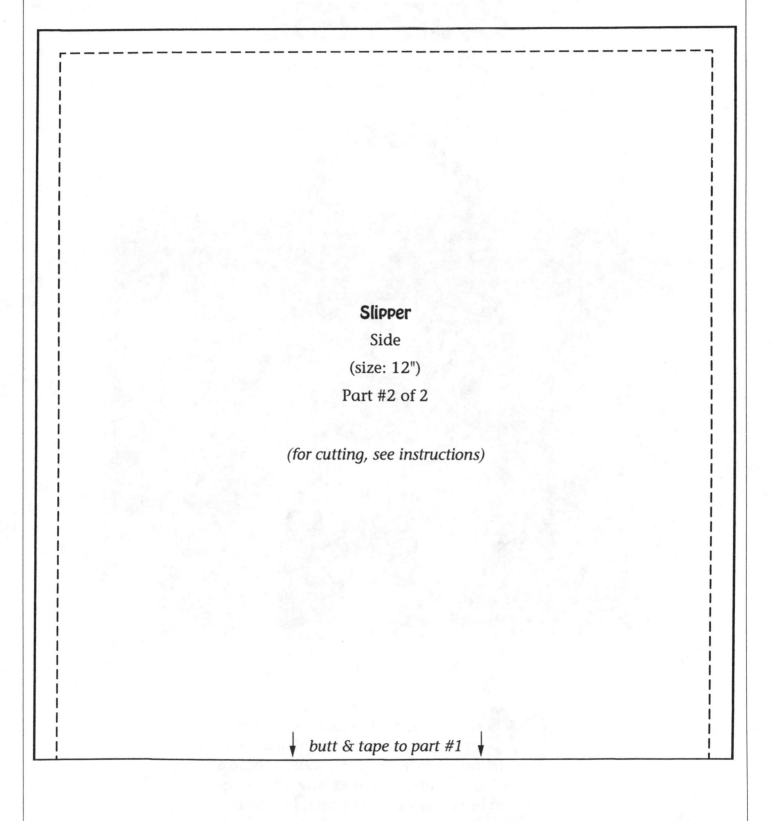

Slipper

Side

(size: 12")

Part #2 of 2

(for cutting, see instructions)

↓ *butt & tape to part #1* ↓

BRIEFCASE

Finished size: 13" x 16½" • Shoulder strap is optional

Made in shades of blacks and grays, or browns, this pieced briefcase means business. For an arty look, choose a colorful mix of fabrics. Either way, this scrap-patched briefcase will prove useful for toting papers, books, or anything of importance.

MATERIALS

³/₄ yard each of five fabrics

Matching thread

Batting scraps

One 22"-long zipper

INSTRUCTIONS

Note: All seam allowances are ¼" unless otherwise specified.

Prewash and iron your fabrics. Prepare patterns as instructed on page 10.

1. Cut the briefcase pieces as follows:

Four body pieces, each

13" x 16½"

Two inside pocket pieces, each 16½" square

Two outside pocket pieces, each 10½" x 16½"

Two bottom/side edges strips, each 3½" x 36½"

Four zipper strips, each 2" x 22"

Using the briefcase pieces as patterns, cut two body pieces, two outside pocket pieces, one bottom/side edges piece, and two top strips from batting.

2. Cut and piece approximately four yards of 1½"-wide bias strips. These are simply strips cut on the diagonal grain (45°) of the fabric.

3. Cut the remaining fabric into 1½"-wide, 2½"-wide, and 2⅞"-wide strips on the straight grain of the fabric. For handles, set aside four 1½"-wide strips, each measuring 20" long. For the shoulder strap, set aside two 36"-long, ½"-wide strips.

Stitch two 1½"-wide strips together.

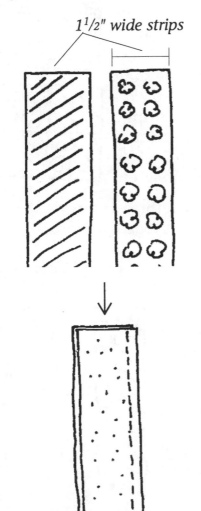

1½" wide strips

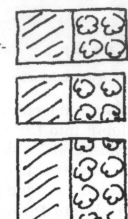

Press the seam allow-ances to one side. Cut the strips into 1½"-long pieces.

Right sides together, match two of these pieces, turning one first, so the fabrics will alternate. Stitch along one edge.

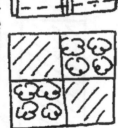

Repeat with two more pieces. Press. Do the same for two 2½"-wide strips. Cut them into 2½"-long pieces.

Stitch three 1½"-wide pieces together. Press.

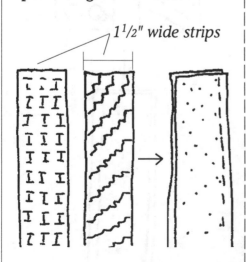

1½" wide strips

Cut the strips into 3½"-long pieces. For the 2½"-wide pieces, cut into 6½"-long pieces.

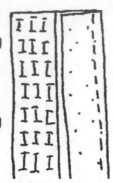

for 1 ½" strips, cut 3½"

for 2 ½" strips, cut 6 ½"

Right sides facing, match two of these pieces, so that the strips are at right angles to one another. Stitch. Repeat for two more pieces. Press the seam allowances to one side. Right sides facing, stitch these two sets together. Press.

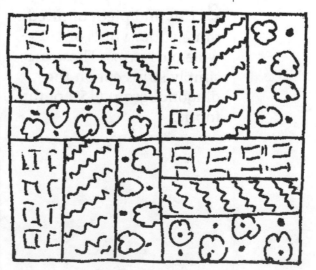

Cut the 2⅞"-wide strips into 2⅞" pieces.

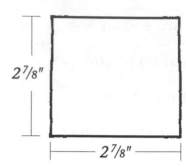

2⅞"

2⅞"

To create triangles, cut from one corner to the diagonal corner for each square.

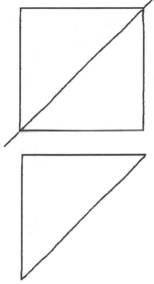

Right sides facing, match two triangles, one of each fabric along the long, diagonal edges. Stitch. Press seam allowances to one side.

Repeat for three more sets of two triangles each. Matching like fabrics, stitch two of these sets together. Press.

Repeat for the two remaining pieces. Right sides facing, stitch these two sets together, matching like fabrics to form a square or set them together to form two rectangles.

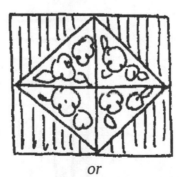

or

Piece together these squares and strips in any order to form two rectangles, each 10½" x 16½".

4. For one handle, stitch two of the strips reserved in step 3 together, right sides facing, along the long edges.

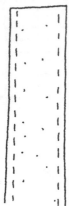

Turn right sides out. Press.

Repeat for the two remaining strips.

5. Press one long edge of an inside pocket piece to the wrong side ¼". Repeat. Topstitch.

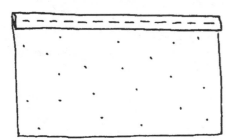

6. Lay one body piece face down on your work surface. Place a matching piece of batting on top. Place a second body piece right side up on top of both of these. Align edges. Pin. Baste the three layers together along all four edges.

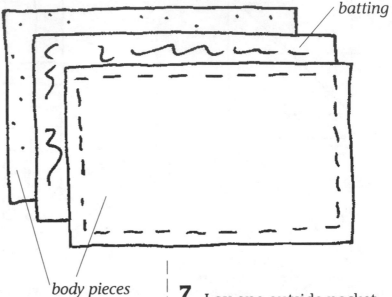

batting

body pieces

Repeat for the other body side of the briefcase.

7. Lay one outside pocket piece right side down. Lay one matching piece of batting on top. Lay the pieced outside pocket right side up on top. Pin around all four edges. Baste.

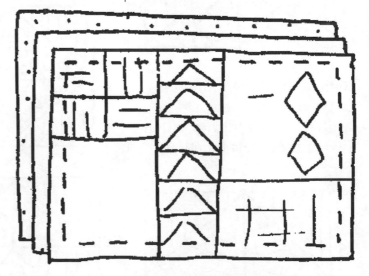

Repeat for the second outside pocket.

9. Lay one outside pocket on top of one body piece, both right sides up. Match the edges as shown. Pin.

Flip the body/ outside pocket over and position the inside pocket, wrong side against the body, as you did the outside pocket. Pin. Baste.

Repeat for the other body and outside and inside pockets.

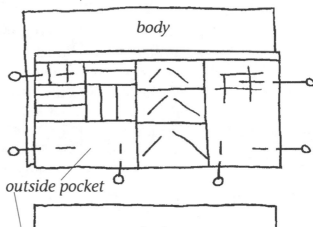

body

outside pocket

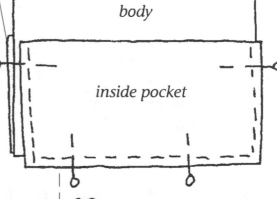

body

inside pocket

8. Apply a piece of bias binding to one long edge of the outside pocket. This will be the top edge of the pocket. First, stitch it to the pieced side of the pocket, right sides facing. Then, fold it as pressed to the inside of the pocket. Topstitch.

10. Position one handle between the body and outside pocket as shown. Have 14" of the strip visible, forming the handle. Stitch two vertical rows through all layers as shown.

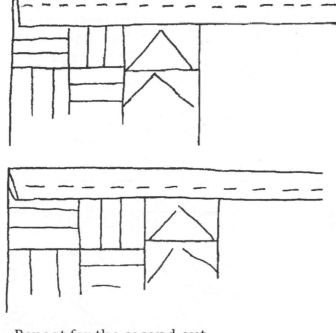

Repeat for the second outside pocket.

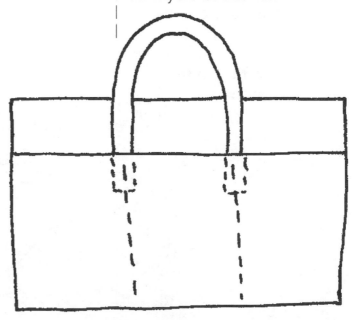

11. Sandwich the batting between the two bottom/side edge strips, with the wrong sides of the fabric against the batting. Baste the raw edges together.

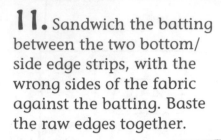

batting

12. Layer the two batting strips against the wrong sides of two zipper strips. Right side of zipper facing right side of fabric, stitch one side of the zipper to one zipper strip and batting.

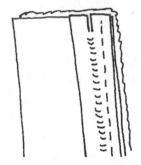

Lay a zipper strip on top and stitch through all layers. Stitch another zipper strip and batting to the other side of the zipper. Stitch the remaining zipper strip on top.

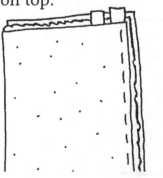

Fold out and baste the raw edges of the sandwich together.

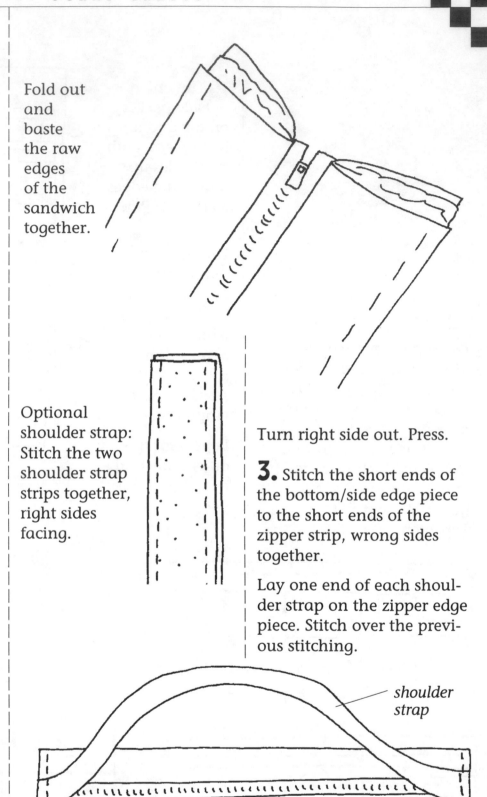

Optional shoulder strap: Stitch the two shoulder strap strips together, right sides facing.

Turn right side out. Press.

3. Stitch the short ends of the bottom/side edge piece to the short ends of the zipper strip, wrong sides together.

Lay one end of each shoulder strap on the zipper edge piece. Stitch over the previous stitching.

shoulder strap

bottom/side edge piece

Cover the raw edges with a bias strip as you did for the top edge of the outside pieced pocket.

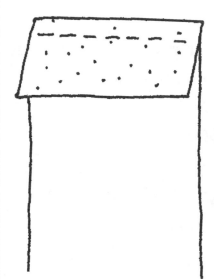

14. Wrong sides together, stitch one briefcase body to one edge of the zipper strip, having the bottom of the pockets on the bottom and the zipper on the top.

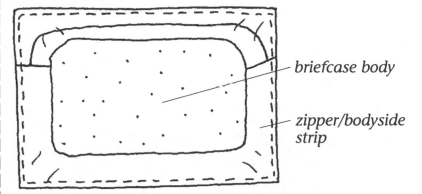

briefcase body

zipper/bodyside strip

Repeat for the other side of the briefcase.

15. Match the raw edges of the bias strips to the raw edges of the briefcase. Stitch. Fold the bias strip over the raw edges. Slip stitch.

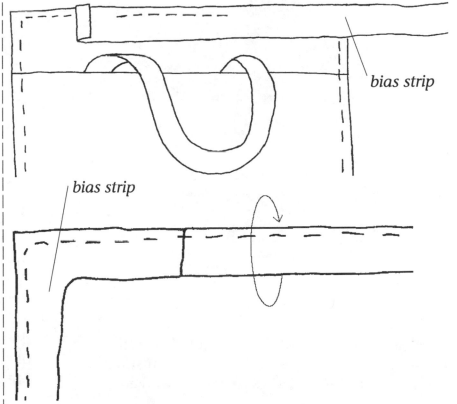

bias strip

bias strip

133

HANDBAG ACCESSORIES

Eyeglass Case

MATERIALS

¼ yard fabric for applique base and lining

Scraps of three different fabrics for appliques

Matching thread

Wonder-Under™

Scrap of batting

INSTRUCTIONS

Note: All seam allowances are ¼".

Prewash and iron your fabrics. Prepare all patterns as instructed on page 10.

1. Cut two pieces of fabric, each 6½" x 8". One will be the applique base, one the lining. Cut a piece of batting the same size.

2. Trace the applique shapes onto the paper backing of the Wonder-Under™. Trace three from each of the three fabrics. Leave about ½" between the shapes. Cut them out about ¼" outside of the traced lines. Following the instructions on the

Keep your eyeglasses scratch free in this attractive little case. Satin stitch applique makes this quick and easy.

Wonder-Under™, fuse to the applique fabrics. Cut out the shapes on the traced lines. To remove the paper backing, slash the paper with the tip of your scissors. Peel paper away.

3. Lay the appliques on the applique base fabric ¼" from the edges. Fuse, following the instructions on the Wonder-Under™.

Arrange diamonds ¼" from edges.

4. Using a machine satin stitch, zigzag stitch over the edges of the appliques.

5. Right sides facing, stitch the two long edges and one short (bottom) edge of the applique base eyeglass case top together.

Repeat for the lining, leaving a 2"-long opening in one side.

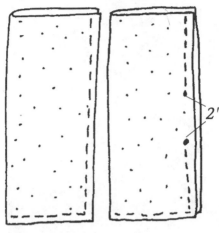

applique base   *lining*

6. Turn the lining right side out. Place inside the applique base. Right sides will be together. Match the top edges. Stitch around top.

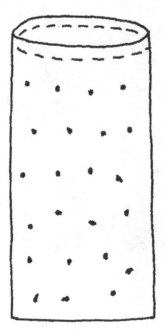

Turn right side out. Topstitch the 2"-long opening in the lining closed.

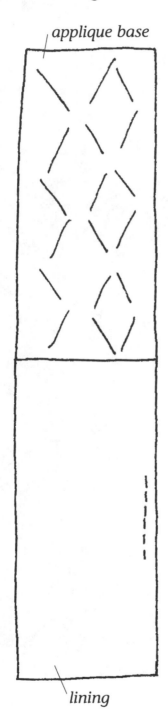

applique base

lining

Put the lining inside the case.

Cosmetic Bag

MATERIALS

¼ yard fabric for the small bag

⅓ yard fabric for the large bag

Scraps of three fabrics for appliques

Matching thread

Wonder-Under™

Scrap of batting

7" nylon zipper for small bag

12" nylon zipper for large bag

Tassel

Instructions are given for two sizes: 4" x 3¾" and 8" x 7½

INSTRUCTIONS

Note: *All seam allowances are ¼".*

Prepare patterns as instructed on page 10.

1. Cut two pieces of fabric, each 6½" x 10½" for the small bag, or 8½" x 15½" for the large bag. One will be the outside applique base of the cosmetic case, one the lining. Cut a piece of batting the same size.

What better way to store your cosmetics in style than with this handy bag. It's a wonderful use for those scrap fabrics from past quilting projects.

2. I used three scrap fabrics with different designs for my applique shapes. For the small bag, I used four appliques from each of the three fabrics. For the large bag, I used eight appliques from each of the three fabrics.

Trace the applique shapes onto the paper backing of the Wonder-Under™. Leave about 1/2" between the shapes. Cut them out about 1/4" outside of the traced lines. Following the instructions on the Wonder-Under™, fuse to the applique fabrics. Cut out the shapes on the traced lines. To remove the paper backing, slash the paper with the tip of your scissors. Peel it away.

3. Lay the appliques on the applique base pieces. Fuse, following the instructions on the Wonder-Under™.

small bag

4. Satin stitch along the raw edges of the applique diamonds in a grid pattern.

small bag

5. Lay appliqued cosmetic bag piece face up on top of the piece of batting. Stitch one side of the zipper to the appliqued piece, as shown, right side of zipper to right side of appliqued piece. The zipper is extra long so you can keep the bottom stop out of your way. You will trim the excess away later.

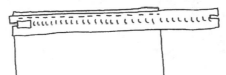

6. Lay one lining piece, right side down, on top, matching the raw edges. Stitch.

Fold these pieces back and repeat for the other side of the zipper and other lining piece.

7. Partially close the zipper. Match and pin the raw edges of the bag as shown. Stitch, leaving a 2"-long opening along one side of the lining for turning.

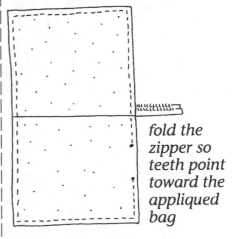

fold the zipper so teeth point toward the appliqued bag

Trim away excess zipper tape. Turn right side out. Topstitch the opening closed.

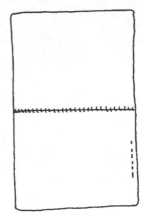

Push the lining into the bag.

8. Handsew the tassel to the zipper pull.

Checkbook Cover

¹/₄ yard fabric for checkbook top and lining

Scraps of three fabrics for appliques

Scraps of Wonder-Under™

Matching thread

Scraps of batting

¹/₂ yard of ³/₄"-wide ribbon

INSTRUCTIONS

Note: *All seam allowances are ¹/₄".*

Prepare all patterns as instructed on page 10.

1. Cut two pieces of fabric, each 8" x 7¹/₂". One will be the checkbook top, one the lining. Cut a piece of batting the same size. Cut two pieces of fabric, each 2¹/₂" x 8". These will be the inside pockets.

2. I used three scrap fabrics with different designs for my applique shapes. Trace the applique shapes onto the paper backing of the Wonder-Under™. Make three appliques from each of the

Add pizzazz to your checkbook with this satin stitch applique cloth cover. It takes just a couple of hours to complete and is the perfect project for any beginning craftsperson.

fabrics. Leave about ¹/₂" between the shapes. Cut them out about ¹/₄" outside of the traced lines.

3. Following the instructions on the Wonder-Under™, fuse to the applique fabrics. Cut out the shapes on the traced lines. To remove the paper backing, slash the paper with the tip of your scissors. Peel it away.

Lay the appliques on the checkbook cover fabric. Fuse, following the instructions on the Wonder-Under™.

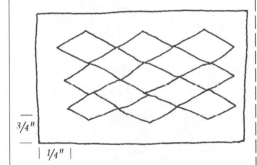

3/4"

| ¹/₄" |

4. Satin stitch along the edges of the appliques.

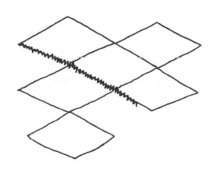

5. Press ¹/₄" to the wrong side on one pocket edge. Repeat. Topstitch.

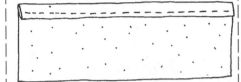

Repeat for the second pocket.

6. Lay the checkbook lining down, right side up. Place the pockets right side down on top, as shown. Pin.

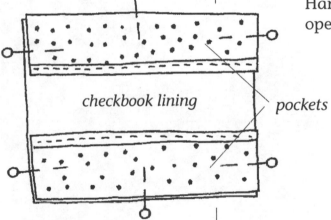

checkbook lining   *pockets*

Cut the ribbon in half. Lay the ribbon along the top edge of the pockets, as shown. Pin.

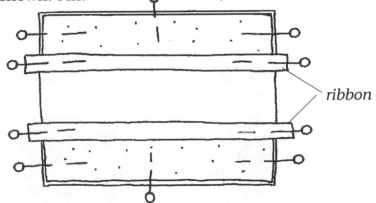

ribbon

Place the checkbook cover right side down on top. Lay the batting on top. Stitch all the way around, leaving a 3" gap in the stitching for turning.

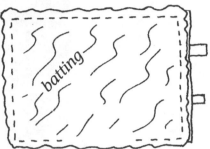

batting

Trim the ends of the ribbon. Trim the corners. Turn right side out. Hand sew the opening closed.

TRAVELING JEWELRY CASE

Protect your favorite jewelry pieces in this soft, fold-away case. Zippered pockets safely stow individual items. Fold it up, tie the tassel, and tuck the bag into a suitcase or drawer.

MATERIALS

3/8 yard fabric applique base and lining fabric

Large scraps for pockets

Scraps of three fabrics for appliques

Matching thread

Batting

Wonder-Under™

Four 12" nylon zippers

1 yard cording, or cording with a tassel at each end

INSTRUCTIONS

Note: All seam allowances are ¼".

Prepare all patterns as instructed on page 10.

1. Cut two pieces of fabric, each 8½" x 17½". One will be the jewelry case top, one the lining. Cut a piece of batting the same size. For the inside pockets, cut two pieces of scrap fabric 2½" x 8½", six 4" x 8½", and two 5½" x 8½". These will be the inside pockets and pocket linings.

2. Trace the applique shapes onto the paper backing of the Wonder-Under™. Make four each from the three applique fabrics. Leave about ½" between the shapes.

Cut them out about ¼" outside of the traced lines. Following the instructions on the Wonder-Under™, fuse to the applique fabrics. Cut out the shapes on the traced lines. To remove the paper backing, slash the paper with the tip of your scissors. Peel it away.

3. Lay the appliques on the jewelry case top fabric. Fuse, following the instructions on the Wonder-Under™.

4. Satin stitch along the edges of the appliques.

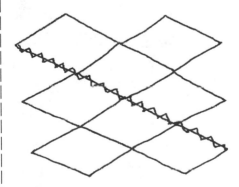

5. Lay one of the 2¹/₂" x 8¹/₂" pieces face up on your work surface. Lay a zipper face down on top. Stitch.

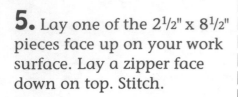

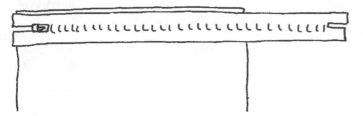

Lay the second strip of the same size face down on top. Stitch.

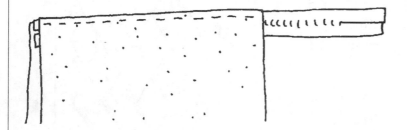

Do the same for the other side of the zipper, using two 4" x 8¹/₂" pieces.

Fold the fabrics back.

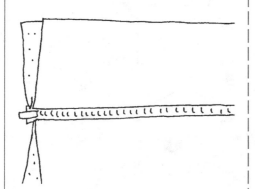

6. Stitch the remaining long raw edge of the first 4" x 8¹/₂" piece to a second zipper, right sides facing.

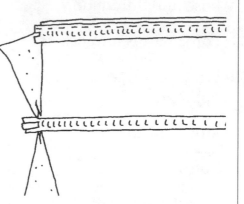

Turn ¹/₄" on the long edge of the other (lining) 4" x 8¹/₂" piece to the wrong side. Fold the zipper out. Topstitch to the zipper.

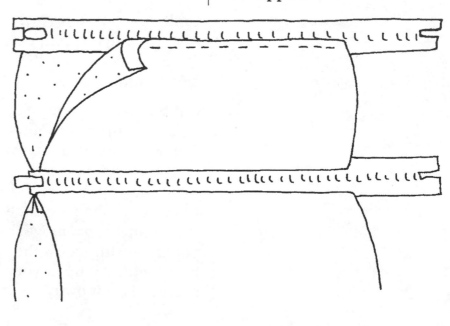

In this same manner add another zipper, then a 4" section for a pocket, a third zipper, and third 4" section. Then add a fourth zipper and a 5½" section for pocket.

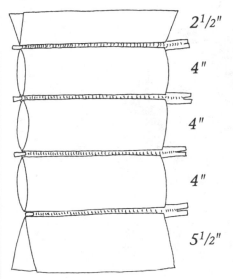

2½"

4"

4"

4"

5½"

7. Wrong side of bag lining facing lining side of pocket assembly, baste the pocket assembly to the remaining 8½" x 17" piece (case lining).

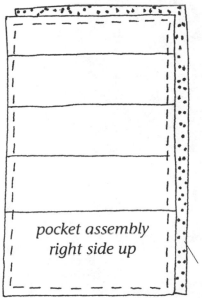

pocket assembly right side up

bag lining, wrong side up

To form pockets, topstitch through all layers as shown.

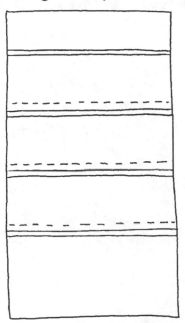

8. Pin the appliqued case top to the pocket assembly, right sides facing.

Fold the cording, as shown. Insert at the top between the two layers.

1/3"

2/3"

Stitch all the way around, leaving a 3" opening for turning. Include the cording in the stitching.

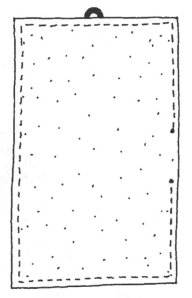

Trim away the excess at the bottom ends of the zippers. Turn right side out. Hand stitch the opening closed.

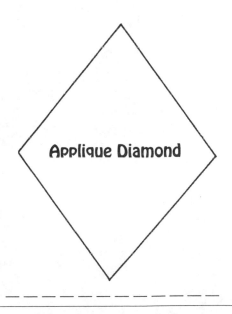

Applique Diamond

143

Crazy-Patched Shoulder Bag

Finished size is 6" x 4".

This convenient little bag is crazy patched from leftover pastel cotton quilting fabrics. A box full of velvet or satin scraps could also be turned into a lovely shoulder bag.

MATERIALS

Fabric scraps

Batting scraps

Matching thread

One 9" nylon zipper

Velcro circles

Embroidery thread

INSTRUCTIONS

Note: All seam allowances are ¼" unless otherwise specified.

Prewash and iron your fabrics. Prepare patterns as instructed on page 10.

1. Lay the pouch and body/flap pattern pieces on the muslin. Cut out muslin rectangles about 1" larger than the patterns. Lay the muslin rectangles on the batting. Cut the batting around the pattern pieces.

2. Crazy patch the pocket, pouch, and body/flap as instructed on page 10. Don't use batting for the pocket.

3. If desired, add embroidery to the crazy patch.

4. Cut one pocket piece, three pouch pieces, and one body/flap piece from the scrap fabric.

5. Right sides facing, stitch the straight top edges of the crazy-patched pocket and a fabric pocket piece together.

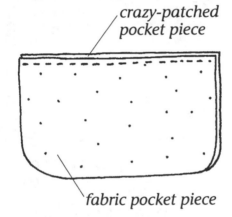

crazy-patched pocket piece

fabric pocket piece

Turn right sides out. Press.

Pin the pocket to the crazy-patched body/flap as shown, crazy-patched sides up. Baste.

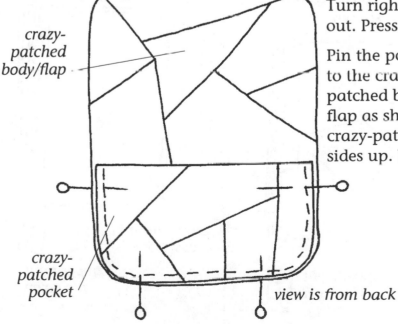

crazy-patched body/flap

crazy-patched pocket

view is from back

145

6. Right sides facing, pin the fabric body/flap lining piece to the crazy-patched body/flap piece. Stitch, leaving a 2" opening along one side for turning.

Turn right side out. Hand stitch the opening closed.

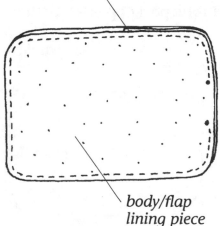

crazy-patched body/flap and pocket

body/flap lining piece

7. Stitch one side of the zipper to the right side of the crazy-patched pouch piece as shown.

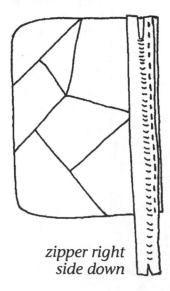

zipper right side down

Lay a fabric pouch piece, wrong side up, on top. Stitch over your previous stitching.

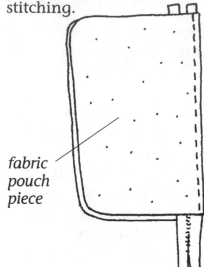

fabric pouch piece

Fold back these pouch pieces. Lay a fabric pouch piece, right side up, on top of the batting pouch piece. Stitch the other side of the zipper to it.

fabric pouch piece with batting beneath

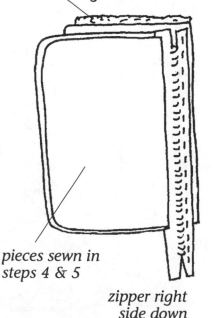

pieces sewn in steps 4 & 5

zipper right side down

Lay the remaining fabric pouch piece, wrong side out, on top. Stitch through all layers.

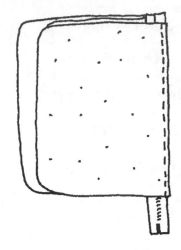

Partially close the zipper. Right sides facing, match and pin the raw edges of the pouch. Stitch, leaving a 2"-long opening along one side for turning as shown.

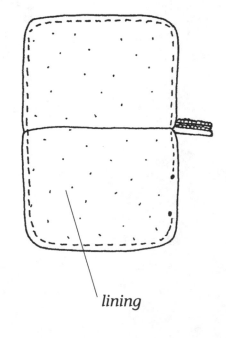

lining

Trim away the extra length of zipper. Turn right side out. Topstitch the opening closed.

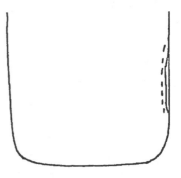

Push the lining into the pouch.

8. Cut a strip of fabric (or piece it) 50" long and 3½" wide. Right sides together, fold and stitch the long sides together. Turn right side out. Fold in half lengthwise. Topstitch ⅛" from each long edge.

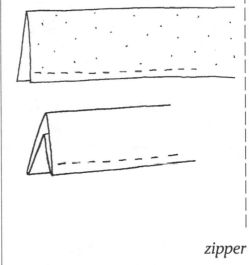

Pin the ends of the ties to the back of the body/flap inside the pocket as shown. Baste.

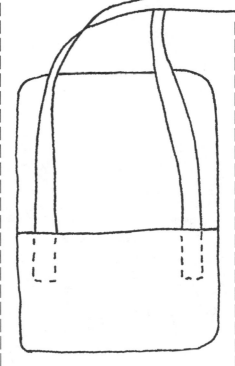

9. Position the pouch on the lining side of the body/flap, on the same end that the pocket (on the back) is on.

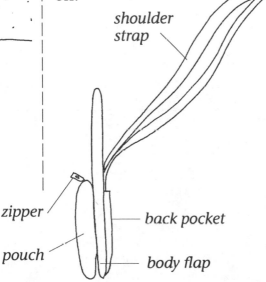

shoulder strap

zipper

pouch

back pocket

body flap

view from back

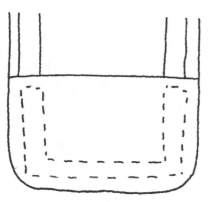

Open the zipper. Stitch through the pouch back, the body/flap, and shoulder strap as shown.

10. Position the velcro on the flap and pouch as shown. Hand stitch.

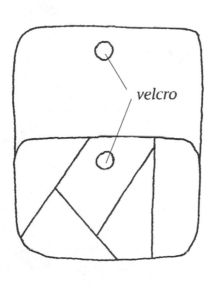

velcro

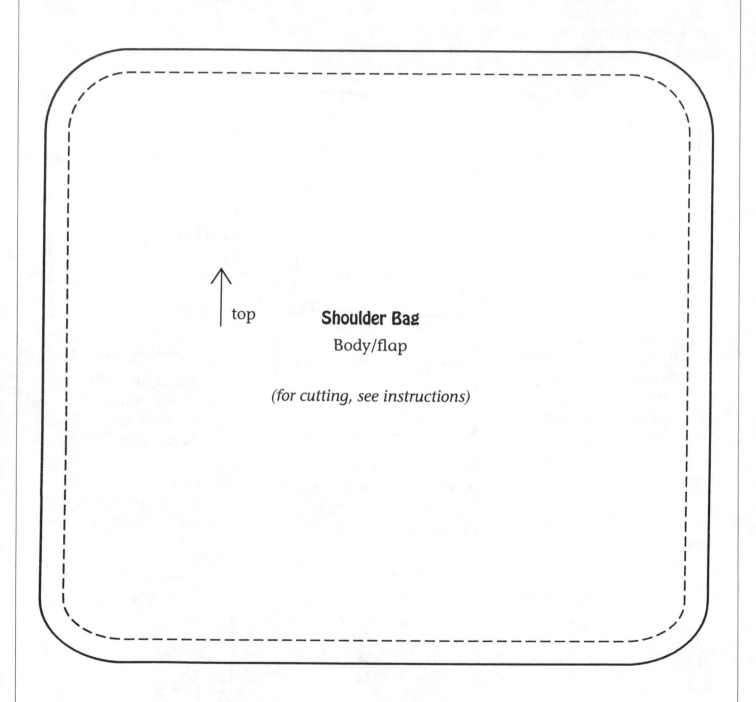

top

Shoulder Bag

Body/flap

(for cutting, see instructions)

Shoulder Bag
Back Pocket

(for cutting, see instructions)

Shoulder Bag
Pouch

(for cutting, see instructions)

FANNY PACK

Finished sizes: Small 6" x 4" • Large 8" x 5¼"

A convenient way to carry small items, this pack is a bit dressier than most fanny packs. Tie it around your waist with a conventional parachute clip, and it will stay at your side all day.

I've provided two sizes: The smaller pack will hold some cash, credit cards, keys, and a lipstick. To accomodate larger items, make the bigger size. Either way, they'll leave your hands free and assure you'll never set down your wallet and leave it behind again!

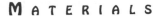 MATERIALS

Fabric scraps

Matching thread

Batting scraps

Zipper: 9" for small,
              12" for large

One parachute clip

One velcro circle

INSTRUCTIONS

Note: All seam allowances are ¼" unless otherwise specified.

Prewash and iron your fabrics. Prepare the patterns as instructed on page 10.

1. Cut the fabric for the woven top into 15 2½" x 10" strips. I chose five fabrics, and made three strips of each.

Right sides together, fold a strip lengthwise and stitch the long edges together.

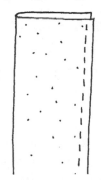

Turn right side out. Press so that the seam is at the back.

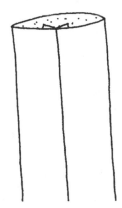

Repeat for the remaining strips.

2. Right sides up, weave the strips, eight in one direction and seven in the other.

3. Lay the body/flap pattern on the woven strips. Trace around the pattern.

Remove. Pin the edges of the strips. Baste. Trim along the marked line.

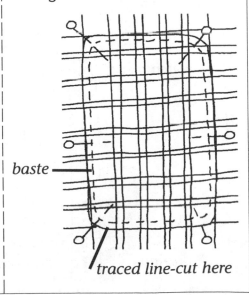

baste

traced line-cut here

4. Lay the fabric body/flap piece, right side down, on top of the woven body/flap. Lay the batting on top. Stitch all the way around, leaving a 4" opening at one short end for turning.

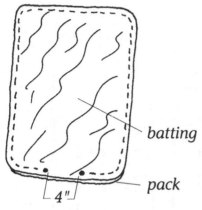

batting

pack

⌐ 4"

Turn right side out. Press.

5. Using one of the pouch pieces as a pattern, cut two pouch pieces from batting. Lay one piece of batting down. Place the pouch piece, right side up, on top. Stitch one side of the zipper, wrong side up, to the pouch/batting.

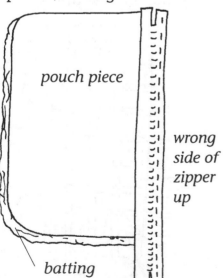

pouch piece

wrong side of zipper up

batting

Lay another pouch (lining) piece on top, wrong side up, matching the raw edges. Stitch.

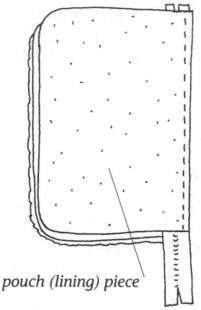

pouch (lining) piece

Fold these layers away from the zipper, into their finished positions.

Likewise stitch the two remaining pouch pieces and one remaining batting piece to the other side of the zipper.

6. Partially close the zipper. Match and pin the raw edges of the pouch. Stitch as shown, leaving a 2"-long opening along one side of the lining for turning.

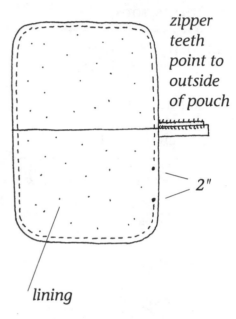

zipper teeth point to outside of pouch

2"

lining

Turn right side out. Trim away the extra zipper. Topstitch the opening closed.

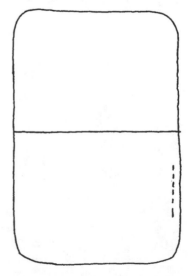

Push the lining into the pouch.

7. Cut two strips of fabric, each 24" long and 2½" wide. Right sides facing, stitch the long sides together. Turn right side out. Press.

Place the ends of the ties on each side of the pouch as shown. Pin.

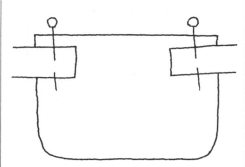

8. Pin the pouch to the body/flap lining (not the woven body/flap), as shown.

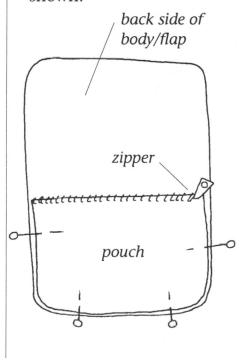

back side of body/flap

zipper

pouch

Hand stitch through the back of the pouch and body/flap lining. Catch the ends of the ties in the stitching.

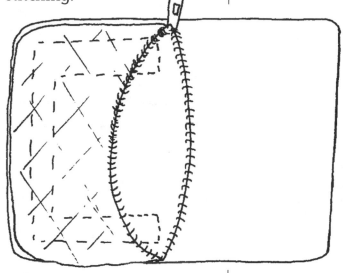

9. For parachute clip fasteners:
Try on the fanny pack. Put the clips on the straps. The clip should be at your back. Pin the straps where the strap comes together at the clip as shown.

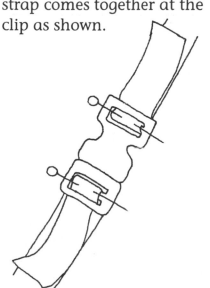

Cut the straps 1½" beyond this point. Remove the pin and the clip. Turn the raw end under ¼". Put the strap back on the clip so that the excess strap will be on the underside (against you) when you are wearing the pack. Stitch as shown.

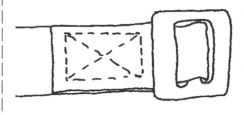

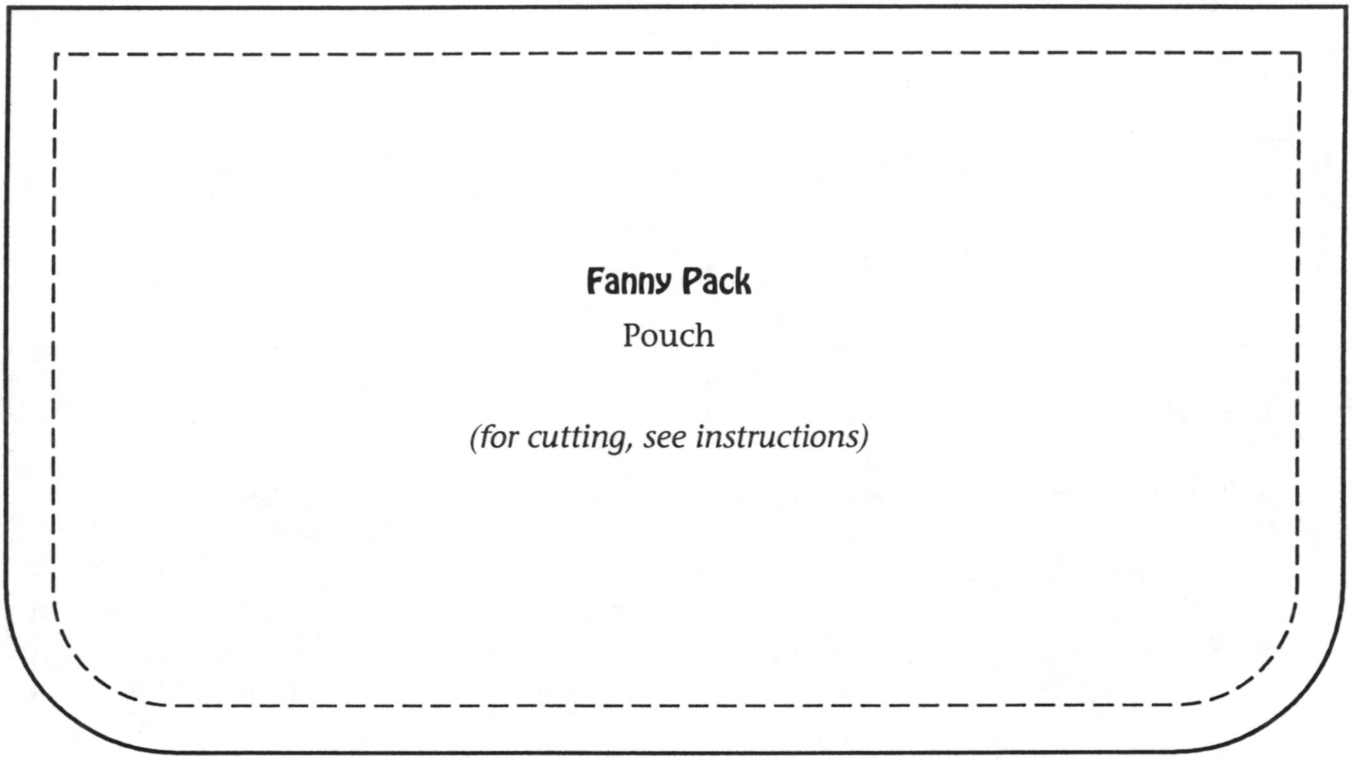

Fanny Pack

Pouch

(for cutting, see instructions)

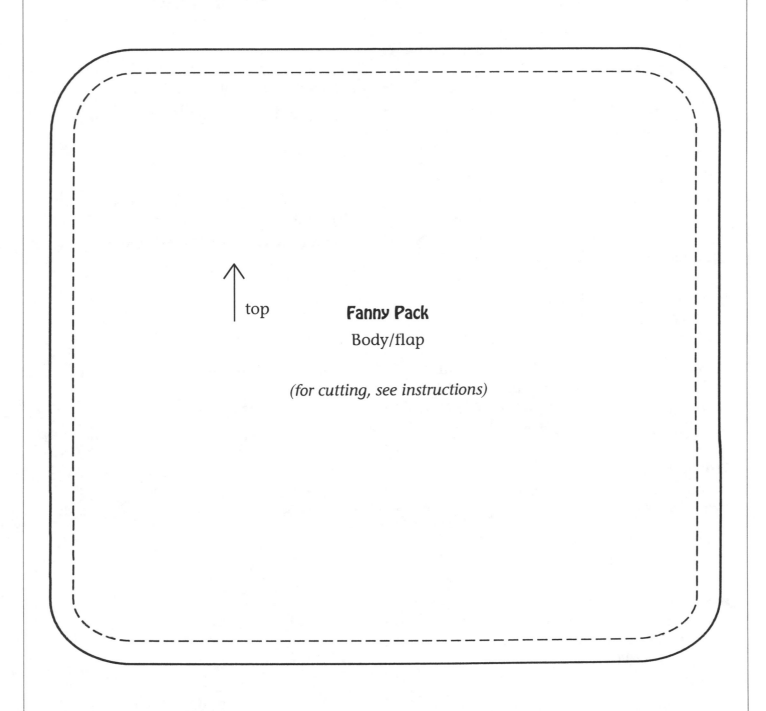

↑ top

Fanny Pack

Body/flap

(for cutting, see instructions)

Sources

CR's Crafts
Box 8
Leland, IA 50453
(515) 567-3652
Catalog: $2

This catalog is full of a large selection of goodies for dollmaking and general crafts.

Clotilde, Inc.
P.O. Box 22312
Ft. Lauderdale, FL 33332
1-800-772-2891
Catalog: $1

Here you will find every sewing notion imaginable, all discounted at least twenty percent. You'll also find the Jiffy Grip™ for the slippers at a great price.

Home Sew
Bethlehem, PA 18018
Catalog: Free

Great source for elastic, lace, trims, and other goodies at fantastic prices.

Keepsake Quilting
Route 25, P.O. Box 1618
Centre Harbor, NH 03226-1618
(603) 253-8731
Catalog: Free

Shop at home with Keepsake's cotton fabric swatch sets. You'll find bias press bars in this catalog.

References

Reader's Digest Complete Guide To Sewing, Readers Digest Books.

An excellent general guide to sewing.

Singer Sewing Reference Library, Cy DeCosse, Inc.

From the basic sewing book to *Quilting By Machine*, I recommend this entire series of full color, heavily illustrated books.

♥ MORE GOOD BOOKS FROM ♥
WILLIAMSON PUBLISHING

To order additional copies of *Easy-To-Make Scrap Crafts*, please enclose $13.95 per copy plus $2.50 shipping and handling. Follow "To Order" instructions on the last page. Thank you.

Easy-to-Make TEDDY BEARS & ALL THE TRIMMINGS
by Jodie Davis

Now you can make the most lovable, huggable, plain or fancy teddy bears imaginable, for a fraction of store-bought costs. Step-by-step instructions and easy patterns drawn to actual size for large, soft-bodied bears, quilted bears, and even jointed bears. Plus patterns for clothes, accessories—even teddy bear furniture!

192 pages, 8½ x 11, illustrations and patterns
Quality paperback, $13.95

Easy-To-Make FAIRY TALE DOLLS & ALL THE TRIMMINGS
by Jodie Davis

Another book in Jodie Davis's ever-popular craft book series shows craftmakers of all abilities how to make adorable, huggable fairy tale dolls. Includes beautiful Cinderella, Little Red Riding Hood with her basket of goodies, Goldilocks and the cuddly Three Bears, and so many more lovable dolls. Step-by-step instructions and illustrations, plus complete patterns-to-size for dolls and their costumes are included.

160 pages, 8½ x 11, illustrations and patterns
Quality paperback, $13.95

Easy-To-Make STUFFED ANIMALS & ALL THE TRIMMINGS
by Jodie Davis

With Jodie Davis's complete and easy instructions, creating adorable stuffed animals has never been easier. Whether you are making gifts for children or additions for a special doll collection, these fuzzy animals are sure to delight anyone. Includes 14-inch unicorn, Rudolph doll, and a large assortment of farm animals — complete with clothing patterns!

208 pages, 8½ x 11, illustrations and patterns
Quality paperback, $13.95

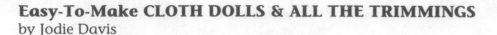

Easy-To-Make CLOTH DOLLS & ALL THE TRIMMINGS
by Jodie Davis

Jodie Davis turns her many talents to making the most adorable and personable cloth dolls imaginable. With her expert directions and clear full-sized patterns, anyone can create these instant friends for a special child or friend. Includes seven 18-inch dolls like Santa, Raggedy Ann, and a clown; a 20-inch baby doll plus complete wardrobe; a 25-inch boy and girl doll plus a wardrobe including sailor suits; and 10 dolls from around the world including a Japanese kimono doll and Amish dolls. Absolutely beautiful and you can do it!

220 pages, 8½ x 11, illustrations and patterns
Quality paperback, $13.95

Easy-To-Make ENDANGERED SPECIES TO STITCH & STUFF
by Jodie Davis

Another wonderful book by the amazing Jodie Davis. Along with making the most adorable stuffed animals such as a loggerhead turtle, spotted owl and bald eagle, you can have wonderful wind socks adorned with these fabulous animals that we all treasure so much. Picture some playful pandas on a black and white windsock or a gorgeous scarlet macaw. And, too, there are instructions for appliqued pillows and beautiful wall-hanging flags of these marvelous creatures. Let Jodie show you how with her step-by-step instructions and full-sized patterns.

192 pages, 8½ x 11, illustrations and patterns
Quality paperback, $13.95

THE BROWN BAG COOKBOOK: Nutritious Portable Lunches for Kids and Grown-Ups
by Sara Sloan

Here are more than 1,000 brown bag lunch ideas with 150 recipes for simple, quick, nutritious lunches that kids will love. Breakfast ideas, too! This popular book is now in its ninth printing as more and more people realize how important every meal is to our health!

192 pages, 8¼ x 7¼, illustrations
Quality paperback, $8.95

GOLDE'S HOMEMADE COOKIES
by Golde Soloway

Over 50,000 copies of this marvelous cookbook have been sold. Now it's in its second edition with 135 of the most delicious cookie recipes imaginable. *Publishers Weekly* says, "Cookies are her chosen realm and how sweet a world it is to visit." You're sure to agree!

162 pages, 8½ x 7½, illustrations
Quality paperback, $8.95

COUNTRY SUPPERS From Uphill Farm
by Carol Lowe-Clay

Gather around the kitchen table, the fireplace, or your favorite picnic spot and enjoy the warm pleasures of country cooking. With Carol Lowe-Clay's newest collection of country recipes, you'll experience authentic farmhouse cooking that is sure to nourish the body as well as the spirit. Sample the savory supper pies, crisp, creative salads, and scrumptious desserts that tempted every palette at Uphill Farm in southern Vermont.

160 pages, 8 x 10, illustrations
Quality paperback, $10.95

THE COMPLETE AND EASY GUIDE TO SOCIAL SECURITY & MEDICARE
by Faustin F. Jehle

A lifesaver of a book for every senior citizen— in fact every citizen—you know.
Do someone a special favor, and give this book as a gift. Written in "plain English," here's all that red tape unravelled. Over 300,000 copies sold! New edition every year!

176 pages, 8½ x 11, charts and tables
Quality paperback, $11.95

CARING FOR OLDER CATS & DOGS: Extending Your Pet's Healthy Life
by Robert Anderson, DVM and Barbara J. Wrede

Here's the only book that will help you distinguish the signs of natural aging from pain and suffering, that will help you care for your pet with compassion and knowledge. How to help your older pet, how to nourish, nurture, and nurse your cat or dog, and finally when and how to let go. Medically sound with reasonable homeopathic remedies, too, mixed with practical advice and compassion. Every older pet deserves an owner who has read this!

192 pages, 6 x 9, illustrations
Quality paperback, $10.95

BUILDING FENCES OF WOOD, STONE, METAL & PLANTS
by John Vivian

Complete how-to on wood fence, stone fence, block, brick, and mud fence, living fence and hedgerows, primitive fence, wire livestock fence, electric barrier fence, and classic horse fence. Next best thing to having a teacher by your side!

224 pages, 8½ x 11, hundreds of drawings, photos, tables, charts
Quality paperback, $13.95

RETIREMENT CAREERS: Combining the Best of Work & Leisure
by DeLoss L. Marsh

Whether your career in retirement is an extension of your life's work, a way to supplement income, a manifestation of a long-time hobby, or a totally new experience, DeLoss Marsh will help you assess your needs and goals to set you forth toward a fulfilling and rewarding retirement.

192 pages, 6 x 9
Quality paperback, $10.95

HOW TO BUILD A MULTI-USE BARN for Garage, Animals, Workshop, or Studio
by John Wagner

Let John Wagner walk you step-by-step through the planning, costing, and building of an all-purpose 30' x 24' barn. Plan the barn's use to meet your special needs. Examines options and modifications in framing and roofing.

192 pages, 8½ x 11, over 100 photographs and illustrations
Quality paperback, $13.95

To order:

At your bookstore or order directly from Williamson Publishing. We accept Visa and MasterCard (please include the number and expiration date), or send check to:

Williamson Publishing Company
P.O. Box 185
Church Hill Road
Charlotte, Vermont 05445

Toll-free phone orders with credit cards: 1-800-234-7891

Please add $2.50 for postage and handling. Satisfaction is guaranteed or full refund without questions or quibbles.